How to answer a JEHOVAH'S WITNESS

ROBERT A. MOREY

BETHANY HOUSE PUBLISHERS
MINNEAPOLIS, MINNESOTA 55438

Published by Bethany House Publishers
A Ministry of Bethany Fellowship International
11400 Hampshire Avenue South
Minneapolis, Minnesota 55438
www.bethanyhouse.com

Printed in the United States of America by
Bethany Press International, Minneapolis, Minnesota 55438

Library of Congress Cataloging-in-Publication Data

Morey, Robert A., 1946–
    How to answer a Jehovah's Witness.

    Bibliography: p.
    1. Jehovah's Witnesses—Doctrinal and controversial works.
2. Witness bearing (Christianity) I. Title.
BX8526.M66   289.9'2   79–25502
ISBN 0–87123–206–5

DR. ROBERT A. MOREY is executive director of the Research and Education Foundation and author of more than thirty books, some of which have been translated into French, German, Spanish, Italian, Finnish, Norwegian, Polish, and Chinese. He is an internationally recognized scholar in the field of comparative religions, the cults, and the occult. His books include:

The Battle of the Gods
Death and the Afterlife
An Examination of Exclusive Psalmody
Fearing God
Here Is Your God
Horoscopes and the Christian
How to Answer a Jehovah's Witness
How to Answer a Mormon
How to Keep Your Kids Drug Free
An Introduction to Defending the Faith
The Islamic Invasion
The New Atheism and the Erosion of Freedom
Reincarnation and Christianity
Studies in the Atonement
The Truth About Masons
When Is It Right to Fight?
Worship Is All of Life
Satan's Devices

Dr. Morey may be contacted at:
Faith Defenders
P.O. Box 7447
Orange, CA 92863

1-800-41-TRUTH

TABLE OF CONTENTS

Part 1

THE CHRISTIAN CHURCH AND THE WATCHTOWER

One of the fastest growing cults today is the Watchtower Bible and Tract Society, or, as it is commonly known, Jehovah's Witnesses. Starting with only 44,080 ministers in 1928, the Watchtower Society peaked at 1,221,504 in 1968.[1]

The growth of the Watchtower is the result of its demand that all of its members be mobilized to evangelize their area, house to house, by selling literature and holding Bible studies. In a recent survey of almost 1,000 members of conservative churches in ten states, we found:

87% had met a Jehovah's Witness.

25% allowed a Witness to come into their home.

23% accepted Watchtower literature.

Almost all contact between members of orthodox churches and Jehovah's Witnesses was the result of a Jehovah's Witness aggressively seeking to convert the orthodox. This answers the question, "From where does the Watchtower recruit its converts?" The Watchtower grows by pulling people out of Christian churches. It is "parasitic" in the sense that it works primarily to win converts who are presently members of established Christian churches.[2]

---

1. The Watchtower, 90:25, January 1, 1969.
2. Gruss, Edmund C., *Apostles of Denial*, Pres. and Ref. Pub. Co., 1970, p. 4.

In the light of this, it is astounding that most pastors receive little or no training to handle Jehovah's Witnesses or to deal with their own parishioners who are about to leave their church to join the Watchtower Society. Theological seminaries do not generally give any training in this area. As a consequence many pastors have felt only fear and confusion when members of their church have suddenly joined the Watchtower and renounced their previous membership.

It is only common sense for pastors to know how to handle the many cultists who are continuously knocking at the front doors of their parishioners. Their people are going to be besieged by cultists at the airport and the local shopping malls. They need to be forewarned and prepared if they are to retain their orthodox beliefs in the present age of the cults and the occult.

Therefore this material is specially designed for pastors or church leaders who desire:

1. To establish their members in the faith to prevent their being converted to the Watchtower.
2. To prepare them to help people out of the Watchtower with a view to their rejoining the Christian Church.

An added incentive for your understanding this work is that the average church member wants his pastor or other church leaders to train him on how to handle the Jehovah's Witnesses who come knocking at his door. He is tired of simply shutting the door on Witnesses. He feels that he should be able to say something to defend his faith. Simply telling lay people not to talk to Jehovah's Witnesses gives credence to the Watchtower's assertion that their arguments are unanswerable. Church members need and desire special training.

That this is true can be seen in the survey already mentioned. We found that:

74% desired special training on what to say to Jehovah's Witnesses.

90% felt that their pastor could and should supply this training.

Of course the average pastor may respond, "Well, I know there is a need and desire for this training in my congregation, *but* I don't have the time or energy to become an expert on the cults and fulfill my pastoral duties at the same time." The exciting thing is that programs are now being developed which will enable the average pastor or church leader to have special instruction on the cults without spending a great deal of time or energy. The material contained in this program can enable any church leader to establish his congregation in the faith and prevent any of them from falling away from Christianity into the Watchtower Society. It does this by putting into the hands of church members a methodology for witnessing to Jehovah's Witnesses.

In going with your people through this material, which is directly aimed at converting Jehovah's Witnesses, your people will be established in the faith so thoroughly that they will never be captured by any of the cults which abound on every hand.

The basic approach and methodology applied here to Jehovah's Witnesses can also be applied to other cults such as the Mormons or the Moonies. A study of the materials will make clear to the leader the fundamental principles and practices involved in dealing with the various cult and occult movements of the twentieth century.

This material has been tested and retested and has been found effective in establishing Christians and converting Jehovah's Witnesses. From this testing we know that this program does not require the presence of an "expert" but depends upon the faithfulness of the average pastor or church leader. The material has been given to congregations in various ways:

1. A special series of Sunday school classes.

2. A two-hour special seminar on Friday evening or on Saturday.
3. Devoting all the Sunday services and calling it "Jehovah's Witness Day."
   a. Sunday school: Ex-Jehovah's Witnesses give testimonies of how and why they left the Watchtower.
   b. Sunday morning: A special sermon on "What to say when Jehovah's Witnesses come knocking."
   c. Sunday evening: The Christian's response to the present rise of the cults and the occult. There can be a panel discussion with questions and answers included.
4. Setting up a special literature display dealing with books and tracts on the cults and the occult.
5. The placing of this program and other titles in the church library as resource material to which members can go.

In the above ways, entire congregations have been instructed in how to deal with the cultists who plead with them to buy their books, blossoms or bags of peanuts.

Where do you start? Begin by reading through the material on your own. Once you are familiar with the program, train your people. You can do it. Your people want you to do it. You must do it to safeguard their souls. Then set up a course of instruction, using the materials which follow as the content of the training.

HOW TO WITNESS TO JEHOVAH'S WITNESSES

At the outset we face a crucial question: "What is the simplest but most efficient way or method of establishing Christians and evangelizing Jehovah's Witnesses?"

By "efficient" we mean that method or plan which:
1. Produces the best results, i.e., establishing Chris-

tians in their faith and producing converts from the Watchtower.

2. Requires the shortest time needed to learn the method.
3. Demands the least energy spent in learning the method and in using it.
4. Avoids unnecessary offense.

By "simple" we mean:

1. Can be understood by the average person, old or young.
2. Can be learned with minimal amount of memorization, little formal education or knowledge of Greek or Hebrew.
3. Can be grasped quickly, retained easily, and used freely.
4. Can be transferred to the average Christian teenager or housewife by a pastor or other leader.

Of what possible use is a plan or method of witnessing to Jehovah's Witnesses which is so complicated that hardly anyone can understand, retain, or use it? Of what use is a plan which requires a knowledge of Greek or Hebrew or the memorization of a detailed refutation of all the texts which the Watchtower twists out of context? If you are the typical pastor, you hardly have time to become an expert in cult apologetics. Your people have even less time. Therefore we need to find a simple but efficient way of establishing Christians and enabling them to respond biblically to Jehovah's Witnesses. We shall now consider the principles which govern such an approach.

Principle I. *Recognize that the real problem which must be dealt with when witnessing to a Jehovah's Witness is the question of religious authority.*

To the average Jehovah's Witness, the Watchtower has the greatest theologians and Bible experts. He is told that the Watchtower has great Greek and Hebrew scholars when in reality they do not have even one such scholar. The Watchtower is "God's visible theocratic organization on earth." It is "God's only channel of truth." The leaders of the Watchtower are "the greatest religious authorities since the Apostles." To question the teaching or the authority of the Watchtower is to be in danger of being disfellow-shipped. You are not to read other religious books. All religious issues are solved in Brooklyn, and nowhere else can the truth be found. The average Witness looks unquestionably to the Watchtower with the same dogmatic devotion that some medieval Roman Catholics had toward Rome and the Pope.

You must recognize that you have no religious authority in the eyes of a Witness. Your religion is of Satan. You pray to Satan. If you doubt this, try praying with a Jehovah's Witness. He will be quick to tell you that he will not and cannot pray with you.

Even the Bible itself has no real authority to a Witness. The Bible *as correctly interpreted by the Watchtower* has authority, but a Witness is trained not to trust himself or others to interpret the Bible.

In the light of this, it is obviously fruitless to battle verse by verse with a Witness. Besides being a waste of great amounts of time, it is not efficient because even if you manage to silence a Witness and to give him arguments which he cannot answer, he will just contact the Watchtower and they *will* give him answers. As long as the Witness trusts the Watchtower as a reliable and faithful guide, you will never get anywhere with him.

Over a period of many years we have had contact with Jehovah's Witnesses who have steadfastly remained in the Watchtower despite their being refuted on many occasions. Fighting with them verse by verse never seemed to get anywhere because the Watchtower headquarters would always come up with an answer. We must remember that the

Watchtower has had 100 years to come up with answers to orthodox arguments. But these Witnesses, once their confidence and trust in the organization was shaken, were brought to salvation.

Principle II. *To destroy the blind obedience and submission which the Jehovah's Witness has toward the Watchtower, you must demonstrate that the Watchtower is not trustworthy or reliable. You must prove that the Watchtower is not "God's visible organization on earth."*

To be quite frank, you must undercut a Witness' trust and confidence in the Watchtower. He must be brought to the realization that he has been deceived by the Watchtower and that, therefore, the Watchtower is not God's religious authority on earth.

Until his confidence in the Watchtower is destroyed, a Witness cannot place his confidence or authority in the Word of God alone. Until he looks to the Bible *alone*, there is no real common ground between you and a Witness.

Principle III. *The simplest and most efficient way of destroying a Witness' blind allegiance to the Watchtower is to show from Scripture and official Watchtower literature that the Watchtower is a FALSE PROPHET. Since it is a false prophet, it is unreliable and not worthy of trust, respect, obedience, or submission.*

It is important throughout your discussion with the Witness that you always place him on your side and stress that the Watchtower is an organization which is trying to deceive both of you. Also always place the wedge *between* the Bible and the Watchtower. It is "us" and "we" against "them." "They" are trying to deceive us." "They" are condemned by the *Bible.* The average Witness is not the false prophet. He has been deceived by the false prophet. So, do not say, *"You* are a false prophet." Rather say, *"The Watchtower* is a *false* prophet and is trying to deceive *you* and *me.* They are condemned by *Scripture* as being a *false* prophet. *We* should not fear or respect them."

How can we establish that the Watchtower is a false prophet? The following steps are a summary of the method which we have found to be quite effective:

Step 1. Establish from Scripture that if someone claims to be a prophet of God the success or failure of their prophecies will determine whether they are a true or false prophet, and whether or not they speak in Yahweh's name. A false prophet will give false prophecies which do not come to pass. A true prophet of God will *always* be infallible in his prophecies. He will be right 100% of the time (Deut. 18:20-22; Matt. 7:15-20). The Watchtower has claimed to be God's inspired prophet who gives prophecies under angelic direction.

Step 2. Deut. 18:20-22 and Matt. 7:15-20 tell us how to judge whether or not the Watchtower is a true or false prophet and whether it truly speaks in Yahweh's name.

Step 3. In 100 years of giving prophecies there has been a 100% failure rate. All the prophecies of the Watchtower have been shown to be false by the passage of time. Time is a false prophet's worst enemy.

Step 4. According to Deuteronomy 18 and Matthew 7, the Watchtower is a false prophet and does not speak in Yahweh's name. The Scriptures command us not to fear, respect, believe or trust the Watchtower.

Step 5. Just as the Watchtower has been false in its prophecies, it is also false in its doctrines. The Watchtower has tried to cover up its false prophecies by willful and deliberate deceit and lies.[3]

Principle IV. *By the above method you will be able to shatter the average Witness' confidence in the Watchtower*

---

3. Van Burskirk, Michael, *The Scholastic Dishonesty of the Watchtower*, CARIS.

as God's only channel of truth today.

Do not argue doctrine, or argue over biblical passages until you have caused the Witness to recognize and to acknowledge that the Watchtower is a false prophet.

The following sections explain how to use the material in this book.

I. *How to Use the Notebook. (Beginning on Page 27)*

The notebook is laid out in a manner to lead a Witness to the conclusion that the Watchtower is a false prophet. This is the only function that the notebook has. You should avoid getting sidetracked to any other topic and strive to share the *entire* notebook with the Witness.

The first section of the notebook establishes the scriptural teaching on the important place of true prophets and their prophecies in the history of redemption. Several Watchtower books are also quoted to hold the Witness' attention and to gain his assent to the scriptural teaching. Make sure you get the Witness' agreement with this material *before* you move on to Section 2. Stay in Section 1 as long as necessary.

Section 2 establishes the fact that the Watchtower has repeatedly claimed to be God's prophet. As you go through the material, have the Witness read out loud the underlined sentences and then ask him to explain what he has just read. Keep pushing the Witness to answer the questions *for himself* from official Watchtower literature. The entire page or article is given just in case the Witness responds by saying, "These quotes are taken out of context." The context is reproduced along with the quote.

Do not be diverted to other topics. Don't discuss whether or not the Watchtower's prophecies have come true. Section 2 establishes only one thing: namely, that the Watchtower has claimed to be God's prophet who gives inspired prophecies received from angels of heaven concerning the future.

Do not proceed to Section 3 until the Witness agrees
that the Watchtower claims to be a "prophet."

Section 3 reproduces from the original sources the many
prophecies of the Watchtower. You must be very careful to
have the Witness first read the questions that are superimposed on the reproduction of the prophecy. Once he has
read the questions, then have him read the underlined por-
tions of the reproduction. If he wishes to read the entire
page, all the better.

Whatever you do, don't bring up whether or not these
prophecies came to pass. Let the Witness do this for himself. If *you* bring it up, he will be on the defensive. *All you
are proving in Section 3 is that the Watchtower "prophet"
has given prophecies concerning the future. What these
prophecies foretold and the dates they involved are the cen-
tral concern.* Don't allow yourself to be trapped into argu-
ing over World War I and 1914. State firmly, "All *we* are
trying to agree on is that the Watchtower has given
prophecies about certain events and dates in the future. We
want to know just what those prophecies are. That's all."

By avoiding a debate on each prophecy's fulfillment,
you will get through all the material and advance to Section 4.

Section 4 is the climax of the notebook. Have the
Witness read out loud the material in this section. Be loving but firm. Constantly place him on *your* side against
that "evil prophet," the Watchtower. Tell him over and
over again that the Watchtower is a false prophet. Point to
Scripture as being the *only* real religious authority.
Transfer his allegiance from the Watchtower to the Bible.

The average Witness has been so brainwashed by the
Watchtower into believing that all other religious organizations are of Satan that he will be tempted to feel, "If the
Watchtower is a false prophet, there is nowhere else to
turn." But you must emphasize the Bible as the place to
which he should turn.

If the Witness seems ready, challenge him to rethink the question of who Christ is. He has never really studied the Bible to answer this question. He has used Watchtower literature to study this issue. If he agrees to study the deity of Christ from the Bible with an open mind, then give him the workbook.

II. *How to Use the Workbook. (Beginning on Page 91)*

The first step is to undermine the reliability of the New World Translation in the mind of a Witness. This can be done in several ways. But the most efficient way is to use two other translations published by the Watchtower. *The American Standard*, 1901 edition, and *The Bible in Living English* are both printed by the Watchtower, though neither was translated by the Watchtower. Get the Witness to use both or either of them.

The workbook is designed for the Witness to answer *for himself* questions concerning the nature of Christ. It would be best for you to go through the study with him. This insures that he will not rationalize his way out of scriptural arguments. But the Witness can work through it alone if he wishes. Either way, keep after him on the subject of the deity of Christ. This is the crucial issue.

What if he brings up the traditional Watchtower arguments and verses? First, remind him that he is repeating something he learned from a false prophet. He should put the Watchtower's teaching aside. Secondly, if he must have an answer to John 14:28; Col. 1:15, etc., tell him, "Write down any verses you are concerned about and then *AFTER* we finish the workbook we will examine them." The main thing is not to get sidetracked into debating over Watchtower texts when he hasn't even had a chance to hear the arguments for the deity of Christ. Once he works through the notebook, he will not be so arrogant; rather, he should be more submissive in spirit. He will thus be in a better mood to hear you out as you untwist the texts which the Watchtower has twisted.

THE WATCHTOWER TEXTS

Once you have finished the workbook, then you can deal with the Witness' list of texts which were given to him to prove that Christ is not God, but a creature, namely, Michael the Archangel. The following is a brief summary of the texts and your answers.

1. Prov. 8:22: This passage refers to "wisdom" and not to Christ. Wisdom in Proverbs is "seeing life from God's perspective." It is pictured as *female* in Proverbs (1:20-23; 2:1-11; 8:1-3). Have him read Prov. 2:1-7 and try putting "Christ" in every place where "wisdom" is mentioned. This does away with his argument in a hurry.

2. John 14:28: Christ said that the Father was "greater" but He did not say "better." The word "greater" refers to work or office while the word "better" refers to nature or essence. As the incarnate servant, the Messiah was not "greater" than the Father, but He willingly subordinated himself to the Father for the purpose of redemption. Christ as *man* would freely say John 14:28. We are proving that Christ is *God* as well as *man*. The Witness must understand that he may prove that Christ was man, but this does not disprove that Christ was God as *well* as man. It is not *either* God or man but *both God and man.*

3. Col. 1:15: "First-born of all creation" does not mean "first one created" any more than "first-born from the dead" means that Christ was "the first one ever resurrected from the dead" (v. 18). "First born" means "the Preeminent One." The text states that Christ created "all things" (vv. 16, 17). He himself cannot be a "thing." The workbook goes into this text in greater detail.

4. Rev. 3:14: "The beginning of the creation of God" should have been and now, in new versions, is translated to

read, "The *origin* of the creation." The Greek word means "origin" or "source."

Further Resource Materials

I. Contact the following counter-cult ministries for a full listing of their materials dealing with the Watchtower:

Narrow Way Ministries
P.O. Box 367
Holbrook, NY 11741

Watchman Fellowship
P.O. Box 7681
Columbus, GA 31908

Witness, Inc.
P.O. Box 597
Clayton, CA 94517

Personal Freedom Outreach
P.O. Box 26062
St. Louis, MO 63136

Those Other Gospels
45 Mulock Place
Harrison, NJ 07029

Alpha and Omega
P.O. Box 47041
Phoenix, AZ 85068

Mt. Carmel Ministries
P.O. Box 5761
Rockford, IL 61125

Take Heed Ministries
P.O. Box 350
Murrysville, PA 15668

II. Recommended books and tapes dealing with Jehovah's Witnesses:

Books by Dr. Robert A. Morey:

Death and the Afterlife, (Minneapolis: Bethany House Publishers)

Battle of the Gods, (Austin: Research and Education Foundation)

The Trinity, (Austin: Research and Education Foundation)

How to Keep Your Faith While at College, (Austin: Research and Education Foundation)

Other Authors:

Duane Magnani, *The Watchtower Files*, (Minneapolis: Bethany House Publishers)

———— , *Dialogue With Jehovah's Witnesses*, (Clayton, CA: Witness)

———— , *Another Jesus*, (Clayton, CA: Witness)

———— , *The Heavenly Weatherman*, (Clayton, CA: Witness)

Gerald Bergman, *Jehovah's Witnesses and the Problem of Mental Illness*, (Clayton, CA: Witness)

Robert Finnerty, *Jehovah's Witnesses on Trial*, (Phillipsburg: P&R)

David Reed, *Jehovah's Witnesses Answered Verse by Verse*, (Grand Rapids: Baker)

———— , *Jehovah's Witness Literature*, (Grand Rapids: Baker)

Audio Tapes by Dr. Robert A. Morey:

How to Witness to Jehovah's Witnesses
Jehovah's Witnesses and the Resurrection of Christ
The Impact of Jehovah's Witnesses
Death and the Afterlife
The Book of Ecclesiastes and Death
The Role of Human Reasoning
God's Love and Eternal Punishment
Dr. Morey Debates a "Soul Sleep" Advocate
Heaven and Hell

Video Tapes by Dr. Robert A. Morey:

How to Witness to Jehovah's Witnesses (Hope
Chapel Series)
Jehovah's Witnesses

Ministries That Minister to Jehovah's Witnesses:

James Bales
707 E. Race
Seacry, AR 72143

Good News Defenders
P.O. Box 8007
La Jolla, CA 92038

Prof. Ed Gruss
P.O. Box 878
Newhall, CA 91322

Equippers, Inc.
4621 Soria Dr.
San Diego, CA 92115

Jehovah's Christian Witnesses
P.O. Box 876
Colorado Springs, CO 80901

CARES
P.O. Box 94
Somers, CT 06071

EMFJ Ministries
2331 Belleair Road #910
Clearwater, FL 34624

Cornerstone Apologetics Team
920 W. Wilson Ave.
Chicago, IL 60640

Sonlight Ministries
P.O. Box 1723
Bellevue, NE 68005

Jesus Is the Truth Ministries
P.O. Box 185
Mount Ephraim, NJ 08059

Jude 3 Missions
P.O. Box 636
Westfield, NJ 07091

Dave Madera
P.O. Box 3040
Long Island, NY 11101

Jude 3
P.O. Box 923
Staten Island, NY 10314

Battleline Ministries
P.O. Box 27402
Columbus, OH 43227

Watchtower Ministries
P.O. Box 2274
North Canton, OH 44720

Charles Trombley
500 N. Elm Place
Broken Arrow, OK 74012

John Warren
22687 S.E. Howlett
Eagle Creek, OR 97022

Witnesses Alive
P.O. Box 25
Forest Grove, OR 97116

Jesus Loves the Lost
P.O. Box 707
Easton, PA 18042

Life After the Watchtower
P.O. Box 251
Elkhart, IN 46515

Ex-Watchtower Slaves for Jesus
P.O. Box 1162
Logansport, IN 46947

Jehovah's Witness Outreach
1298 33rd St.
Cedar Rapids, IA 52402

Promises Kept
1544 Apple Lane
Ottawa, KS 66067

Jehovah's Kingdom Ministries
310 W. Atkinson
Pittsburg, KS 66762

Paul Blizard
P.O. Box 607
Fairdale, KY 40118

David Reed
P.O. Box 840
Stoughton, MA 02072

Gospel Truths Ministries
P.O. Box 1015
Grand Rapids, MI 49501

Steve Huntoon
P.O. Box 1474
Jackson, MI 49204

Christian Ministries, Intl.
7601 Superior Terrace
Eden Prairie, MN 55344

Doorstep Ministries
P.O. Box 7351
Rochester, MN 55901

William Alnor
P.O. Box 11322
Philadelphia, PA 19137

Watchman Fellowship
P.O. Box 14482
Arlington, TX 76094

Joe Hewitt
P.O. Box 279
Fate, TX 75032

Eric Grieshaber
2715 Old Jacksonville Hwy.
Tyler, TX 75701

JW Research
2011 Virginia Ave.
Everett, WA 98201

MacGregor Ministries
P.O. Box 591
Point Roberts, WA 98281

Part 2

THE WATCHTOWER, THE WORD OF GOD, AND PROPHECY

1. THE WORD OF GOD AND PROPHECY

How did God reveal to man the future of this world? How did God reveal His will, plan, and truth for this age?

> God, having of old time spoken unto the fathers in the prophets . . . for no *prophecy* ever came by the will of man: but *men spake from God, being moved by the Holy Spirit.* (Heb. 1:1; 2 Pet 1:21)

According to Scripture, God revealed His will, truth, and the future of this world to us through a special group of men called "prophets."

In *Aid to Bible Understanding* (p. 1347), a "prophet" is defined as "One through whom Divine will and purpose are made known." The "prophecy" given by the prophet is defined as "an inspired message: a revelation of divine will and purpose" (p. 1344). It is further stated in *Aid to Bible Understanding* (p. 1344):

> The source of true prophecy is Jehovah God. He transmits it by means of His Holy Spirit or, occasionally, by Spirit-directed angelic messengers.

It is clear that we must listen to God's prophet, for whatever he says comes from God himself. Is it any wonder then that Moses warned of God's judgment if we reject His prophet? (Deut. 18:18, 19).

But we are aware of the fact that there are many "prophets" around today, all claiming to speak in God's name. We must ask the question set forth in Deut. 18:21:

> And if thou say in thy heart, "How shall we know the word which Jehovah hath not spoken?"

Has YHWH given us a test by which we can distinguish between true and false prophets? In answer to the question posed in Deut. 18:21, Moses himself gives us the test in verse 22:

> When a prophet speaketh in the name of Jehovah, if the thing follow not, nor come to pass, that is the thing which Jehovah hath not spoken: the prophet hath spoken it presumptuously, thou shalt not be afraid of him.

The supreme test to identify a false prophet is to see if his prophecies come true. If his prophecies fail to come to pass, Moses commands us not to be afraid of him:

> But the prophet, that shall speak a word presumptuously in my name, which I have not commanded him to speak, or that shall speak in the name of other gods, that same prophet shall die. The prophet hath spoken it presumptuously, thou shalt not be afraid of him. (Deut. 18:20, 22)

In agreement with the teaching of Moses, Jesus also points out in Matt. 7:15-20 the supreme test to distinguish between true and false prophets:

> Beware of false prophets, who come to you in sheep's clothing, but inwardly are ravening wolves. By their fruits ye shall know them. Do men gather grapes of thorns, or figs of thistles? Even so every good tree bringeth forth good fruit; but the corrupt tree bringeth forth evil fruit. A good tree cannot bring forth evil fruit, neither can a corrupt tree bring forth good fruit. Every tree that bringeth not forth good fruit is hewn down, and cast into the fire. Therefore by their fruits ye shall know them.

The "fruits" of the tree are the prophecies of the prophet in question. Just as a good tree NEVER bears evil fruit, a true prophet NEVER gives a false prophecy. Jesus said, "By their fruits [prophecies] ye shall know them."

In *Aid to Bible Understanding* (p. 1348), we read:

> The three essentials for establishing the credentials of the true prophet, as given through Moses were: the true prophet would speak in Jehovah's name; the things foretold would come to pass (Deut. 18:20-22); and his prophecies must promote true worship, being in harmony with God's revealed Word and commandments. (Deut. 13:1-4)

In agreement with this, *Make Sure of All Things, Hold Fast To What Is Fine*, gives Deut. 18:21-22 as the scripture reference under the heading, "Distinguishing Between True and False Prophets."

In the October 8, 1968 *AWAKE!*, there appeared an article entitled, "A Time to 'Lift Up Your Head' in Confident Hope." It stated on page 23:

> True, there have been those in times past who predicted an "end to the world," even announcing a specific date. Some have gathered groups of people with them and fled to the hills or withdrawn into their homes waiting for the end. Yet, nothing happened. The "end" did not come. They were guilty of false prophesying. Why? What was missing?

> Missing was the full measure of evidence required in fulfillment of Bible prophecy. Missing from such people were God's truths and the evidence that he was guiding and using them.

SUMMARY

God's will, truth, and plan for the future of this world was revealed through prophets. A true prophet proved that he spoke as the messenger of God by giving true prophecies concerning the future. His prophecies always came true. A false prophet, even though he spoke in Jehovah's name, gave false prophecies which failed to come to pass. The supreme test for all prophets according to Moses and Jesus is whether their prophecies come true.

2. THE WATCHTOWER AND GOD'S PROPHET TODAY

Has the Watchtower ever claimed to be Jehovah's prophet today? Is the Society "the Servant of Jehovah" who proclaims inspired prophecies received from angelic communication? Is the Watchtower "God's channel" and "God's messenger" today?

Let the reader answer these questions honestly for himself/herself by examining the following pages wherein they will find photostatic reproductions of official Watchtower literature. The entire page or article has been reproduced in order to give the context to what the Society says concerning itself. The questions, superimposed on the reproductions, are the author's.

As a result, you will be "like a tree planted by streams of water," ever fruitful and ever green, and 'everything you do will succeed.'—Heb. ... 1-3; ...

¹⁹ D... expres... as Dav... ...nstruct me, O Jehovah, in

your way, and lead me in the path of uprightness on ... ." In harmony ... ur whole ... Creator's ... sappoint- ... will not end in heartache. "Take exquisite delight in Jehovah, and he will give you the requests of your heart."—Ps. 27:11; 37:4; see also Philippians 4:6, 7.

What do we need today?
What will God's spokesman tell us?

19. What request should we make to Jehovah, and with what assurance?

T HERE is a real need today for someone to speak as a true representative of God. Why?

Because things are taking place that people do not understand —things that greatly affect their daily activities, yes, their very lives. The churches do not have a satisfactory explanation. But God does have. Is there someone who can bring the truth of God's Word to the people, letting them know what is ahead and what they can do for safety and survival?

We can better understand what is taking place by going back to something described in the Bible that took place under conditions very similar to today's situation. By seeing what God did then, and for what reasons, we can discern what he is doing today, and where we fit in. We can be sure that our discernment will thus be accurate, for God never changes his principles. The way he viewed matters back there is the way that he views similar matters now.—Mal. 3:6.

In the situation referred to in the past a messenger was needed, and one was found and commissioned. He was a Jewish servant of God, the priest Ezekiel. Ezekiel was living when his people, the Jews, were in a sad condition. The year was 613 B.C.E., and Ezekiel was with some of his

WANTED
A Messenger

countrymen in exile in Babylonia. But the majority of the Jews were yet back in Jerusalem and the land of Judah, and though they were unaware of it, they were facing great danger. For this reason, most of the message delivered by Ezekiel, though he was in Babylonia, was a warning to the Jews remaining in Jerusalem, reinforcing a like message being delivered by the prophet Jeremiah in Jerusalem itself. But Ezekiel's message also served to correct the Jews in Babylonia as to their attitude toward God.

Jehovah God appeared to Ezekiel in a vision in which he beheld the celestial chariot of Jehovah. (Ezek. chap. 1) Overwhelmed to the point of prostrating himself before the "likeness of the glory of Jehovah," Ezekiel heard the voice of the chariot's Rider commissioning him.

Jehovah addressed Ezekiel, not by his personal name, but as "son of man." By this expression, in Hebrew ben adám, the Most High God called attention to Eze-

32

kiel's lowly state and origin, as but an offspring of earthling man. The prophet's own name, therefore, receives no prominence in the prophecy.

We are not to understand this addressing of Ezekiel as "son of man" to mean that he was a "type" of Jesus Christ, who spoke of himself seventy-six times as "the Son of man." In Jesus' case, he was comparing himself, not with Ezekiel, but with the "son of man" seen in vision in Daniel 7:13. That "son of man" received kingly authority from God.—Compare Acts 7:56.

EZEKIEL COMMISSIONED

As Ezekiel lay prostrate on the ground, Jehovah said to him: "Son of man, stand up upon your feet that I may speak with you." God's command imparted active force to Ezekiel: "And spirit began to come into me as soon as he spoke to me, and it finally made me stand up upon my feet that I might hear the One speaking to me." (Ezek. 2:1, 2) The serious need for a messenger was then revealed to Ezekiel, God saying:

"Son of man, I am sending you to the sons of Israel, to rebellious nations that have rebelled against me. They themselves and their forefathers have transgressed against me down to this selfsame day. And the sons insolent of face and hard of heart—I am sending you to them, and you must say to them, 'This is what the Sovereign Lord Jehovah has said.' And as for them, whether they will hear or will refrain—for they are a rebellious house—they will certainly know also that a prophet himself happened to be in the midst of them."—Ezek. 2:3-5.

Ezekiel was thereby commissioned. Note that he did not raise himself up to be a prophet. This difficult mission was not one an individual was likely to choose for himself. The fact that Jehovah appeared to him in a remarkable vision (and later in the vision revealed things to him that could not otherwise have been known by Ezekiel), also that Jehovah commissioned

him directly—all these things prove that what Ezekiel said and wrote in his prophecy was inspired by Jehovah. He was in an outstanding way made a witness of Jehovah God. His being a witness of Jehovah is emphasized by his unusually frequent use of God's personal name.

EZEKIEL PROPHETIC OF A GREATER MESSENGER

Moreover, not only were Ezekiel's words prophetic, but also he was a prophetic figure in his action, as shown on occasion. (Ezek. 24:24) He was a "portent" or sign. Of whom was he—this messenger—a prophetic figure, since he did not prefigure Jesus Christ? Consider first this evidence.

It was only about six years after Ezekiel's vision of God's celestial "chariot," namely, in 607 B.C.E., that Jerusalem was destroyed by the armies of King Nebuchadnezzar of Babylon. So, if the evidence shows that Ezekiel was a prophetic figure of a 'messenger' of God today, this world's system of things does not have much longer before its complete end. Certainly the world would need a God-sent messenger to give warning.

Indications are that since 1914 this world has been in its 'time of the end.' Modern historians are agreed that an era ended in that year when World War I began its violent, destructive course. They have arrived at this conclusion without realizing that the Bible's chronology marks 1914 as the date for the end of the "times of the Gentiles."—Luke 21:24, *Authorized Version.*

How does the Bible show 1914 to be a marked date? Why is it of such great importance? Because it has to do with God's exercise of his sovereignty toward the earth. Up to the time of Jerusalem's fall to Neouchadnezzar, God had expressed his sovereignty over part of the earth, that is, the domain of the kings of Judah, through

Covenant of the League of Nations was made a part of that peace treaty.

When the League of Nations was proposed as an international organization for world peace and security, the bloodstained religious organizations backed it, seizing upon this circumstance as an opportunity to "save face." The Church of England and the churches of Canada supported the League, since Great Britain was the League's proposer and chief backer. In the United States of America there was the Federal Council of the Churches of Christ in America (superseded in 1950 by the National Council of the Churches of Christ in the U.S.A., a federation of 33 Protestant and Orthodox churches). On December 18, 1918, this Council sent its adopted Declaration to the American president and urged him to work for the League. The Declaration said, in part:

> "Such a League is not a mere political expedient; it is rather the political expression of the Kingdom of God on earth. . . . The Church can give a spirit of good-will, without which no League of Nations can endure. . . . The League of Nations is rooted in the Gospel. Like the Gospel, its objective is 'peace on earth, good-will toward men.'"

By accepting the League of Nations as "the political expression of the Kingdom of God on earth," the members of the Federal Council of churches were really accepting a counterfeit "Kingdom of God on earth." Why? Because Jesus Christ, the Head of the church, when on trial for his life before the Roman governor Pontius Pilate, in 33 C.E., said: "My kingdom does not belong to this world. If it did, my followers would be fighting to save me from arrest by the Jews. My kingly authority comes from elsewhere." (John 18:36, *New English Bible*) The fact that they were not, as a body, a commissioned messenger of God was made clear and their hypocrisy exposed when, twenty years later, the League of Nations was knocked out of

business by the outbreak of World War II. The churches again entered into this war with all their might, encouraging their members to take part.

WHAT IS REQUIRED OF GOD'S MESSENGER

Therefore, when it came time for the name of Jehovah and his purposes to be declared to the people, along with God's warning that Christendom is in her "time of the end," who qualified to be commissioned? Who was willing to undertake this monumental task as Jehovah's "servant"? Was there anyone to whom Jehovah's heavenly "chariot" could roll up and whom it could confront? More accurately, was there any group on whom Jehovah would be willing to bestow the commission to speak as a "prophet" in His name, as was done toward Ezekiel back there in 613 B.C.E.? What were the qualifications?

Certainly such a messenger or "servant" group would have to be made up of persons who had not been defiled with blood-guilt as had Christendom and the rest of Babylon the Great, the world empire of false religion, by sharing in carnal warfare. In fact, they would be a group that had come out from the religious organizations of Babylon the Great. More than that, they would be persons who not only saw the hypocrisy and God-defaming action of these religions, but in addition actually rejected them and turned to Jehovah God in true worship of him as set forth in the Bible. Who would they be?

In identifying the group that is truly commissioned as God's messenger, these are points for us to consider seriously. God does not deal with persons who ignore his Word and go according to their own independent ideas. Nor does he recognize those who make a profession of serving him and at the same time associate with religions that teach God-dishonoring doctrines. No one can serve two masters, claiming to be a worshiper of God and meddling with the politics, the radical movements and other schemes of this world. (Matt. 6:24) Jehovah's chief representative, Jesus Christ, said: "Not everyone saying to me, 'Lord, Lord,' will enter into the kingdom of the heavens, but the one doing the will of my Father who is in the heavens will."—Matt. 7:21.

It is of importance to every individual on earth to identify the group that Jeho-vah has commissioned as his "servant" or messenger. We must recognize and understand the warning that he brings. We need to take action on the warning to safeguard our lives, for they are in a danger as grave as that of the lives of Jerusalem's citizens as that city neared destruction. For this reason forthcoming issues of The Watchtower will further discuss the identity and work of Jehovah's commissioned messenger as revealed in His vision to Ezekiel.

● Why did the Mosaic law prohibit the eating of fat?—U.S.A.

Under the Law given to the Israelites, both the blood and the fat were considered as belonging exclusively to Jehovah God. The Law stated: "It is a statute to time indefinite for your generations, in all your dwelling places: You must not eat any fat or any blood at all." —Lev. 3:17.

The blood represents the life of a person or an animal. For this reason the Bible speaks of the "soul" as being "in the blood." (Gen. 9:4; Lev. 17:11, 14) Since only Jehovah God can give life, life or that which represents life, the blood, rightly belongs to him.

The fat was regarded as the best or richest part. This is evident from such figurative expressions as the "fat part of the land," "the best [literally, the fat] of the oil," and "the best [literally, the fat] of the new wine and the grain." (Gen. 45:18; Num. 18:12) Thus the prohibition against eating fat evidently served to impress upon the Israelites that the "first" or best parts belong to Jehovah, to be offered up to him in sacrifice. The eating of fat would therefore have been an illegal appropriation of something that had been sanctified to Jehovah. It would have been an invasion of his rights. However, in the case of an animal that died of itself or was killed by another beast, fat could be used for other purposes.—Lev. 7:23-25.

Many Bible commentators believe that the command about fat pertained only to animals acceptable for sacrifice. But there are indications that this prohibition against eating fat applied to the fat of all animals. The injunction respecting fat is linked with the one regarding blood. And the blood of all animals was prohibited for food. (Lev. 17:13, 14; Deut. 12:15, 16) Reasonably, therefore, the regulation regarding fat likewise embraced the fat of all animals.

It may also be noted that proper bleeding did not remove every molecule of blood from the meat, and yet the residue of blood remaining did not make the meat unfit for consumption. Similarly, the prohibition on the eating of fat did not render meat with traces of fat unsuitable for food.

Of course, the prohibition on fat did not rule out the feeding or fattening of sheep or cattle for the table. The Scriptures even mention "fattened cuckoos." (1 Ki. 4:23) In view of the restriction on the use of fat for food, evidently the 'fattening' was not for the purpose of producing layers of fat, but that the animals might become full-fleshed, not skinny.

At Deuteronomy 32:14 the reference to the "fat of rams" as being given to the Israelites is figurative. It designates the best of the flock (similar to the English expression "the cream of the crop"). Hence The Jerusalem Bible reads, "rich food of the pastures." The words of Nehemiah 8:10, "Go, eat the fatty things," are to be understood similarly. The "fatty things" figuratively denote rich, luscious

'They shall know that A PROPHET

Does Jehovah have a prophet to help us today?
Who is this prophet?
How can we prove the identity of God's prophet?

JEHOVAH GOD is interested in having people know him. Though he is invisible to human eyes, he provides various ways by which they can know his personality. They can know what to expect from him and what he expects of them.

One can come to understand that Jehovah is a God of surpassing wisdom by observing creation. This also reveals the loving care with which he designed things for man's welfare and enjoyment. A second way to know God is through his Word of truth, the Bible. Herein one finds the full expression of Jehovah's purpose toward mankind—why man is on the earth and the blessings that God has in store.

A third way of coming to know Jehovah God is through his representatives. In ancient times he sent prophets as his special messengers. While these men foretold things to come, they also served the people by telling them of God's will for them at that time, often also warning them of dangers and calamities. People today can view the creative works. They have at hand the Bible, but it is little read or understood. So, does Jehovah have a prophet to help them, to warn them of dangers and to declare things to come?

IDENTIFYING THE "PROPHET"

These questions can be answered in the affirmative. Who is this prophet? The clergy of the so-called "Christian" nations hold themselves before the people as being the ones commissioned to speak ... as pointed ... evious issue ... azine, they ... God and ... claimers of ... by approving a man-made political organization, the League of Nations (now the United Nations), as "the political expression of the Kingdom of God on earth."

However, Jehovah did not let the people of Christendom, as led by the clergy, go without being warned that the League was a counterfeit substitute for the real kingdom of God. He had a "prophet" to warn them. This "prophet" was not one man, but was a body of men and women. It was the small group of footstep followers of Jesus Christ, known at that time as International Bible Students. Today they are known as Jehovah's Christian witnesses. They are still proclaiming a warning, and have been joined and assisted in their commissioned work by hundreds of thousands of persons who have listened to their message with belief.

Of course, it is easy to say that this group acts as a "prophet" of God. It is another thing to prove it. The only way that this can be done is to review the record. What does it show?

During the World War I period this group, the International Bible Students, was very active in preaching the good news of God's kingdom, as their Leader Jesus Christ had set this work before them in his prophecy at Matthew 24:14. They took literally Jesus' words to the Roman governor Pontius Pilate: "My kingdom is no part of this world." (John 18:36) They also took to heart Jesus' words to his followers: "You are no part of the world, but I have chosen you out of the world." They expected to suffer for living according to that rule, just as Jesus went on to say, "on this account the world hates you." (John 15:19) Hatred toward them grew into violence during World War I.

These Bible Students had long been concerned with Ezekiel and his prophecy. In 1917 they published a book entitled "The Finished Mystery," explaining the book of Ezekiel as well as that of Revelation. This book criticized the clergy as false to the Word of Jehovah. Within nine months a ban was put on its circulation in the United States and Canada. Then eight members of the Watch Tower Bible and Tract Society, including its president and secretary-treasurer, were sentenced to prison in the Federal penitentiary, Atlanta, Georgia, U.S.A.

Though the work of these Christians was crippled for a while, after only nine months the eight men were freed from prison, in March 1919. They accepted this as an answer from God to their prayers. Their work was revived, much to the consternation of the clergy, who had been behind the banning.

Accordingly, their magazine *The Watch Tower and Herald of Christ's Presence,* in its issues of August 1 and 15, 1919, encouraged vigorous resumption of the work of preaching the good news free from the fear of men. Under the subject "Blessed Are the Fearless," the following statements were made:

"There is a fear which is very proper, and which everyone must have who is pleasing to God, and this is known as 'Godly fear'. It means a holy reverence for Jehovah and a fear lest we should displease him and come short of the blessings he has promised us. . . . The Scriptures abound with testimony that those whom God approves do not fear man nor any other creature, but have a holy, reverential fear of Jehovah. In times of old Jehovah justified some men to friendship with him, and the record of his dealing with them was written for the benefit of the church."

Ezekiel was one of these men so used by God, and not only his prophecies, but also Ezekiel himself and his acts were pictorial of things to come.

THE "PROPHET" SPEAKS TO CHRISTENDOM

A General Convention was held by the International Bible Students at Cedar Point, Ohio, September 1-8, 1919. Thousands of Jehovah's servants were present from the United States and Canada. There the Watch Tower Society's president urged the fearless resumption of the work, and this with the use of the outspoken magazine entitled "The Golden Age." In the public talk delivered on the subject "The Hope for Distressed Humanity," the speaker declared that the Lord's displeasure was certain to be visited upon the League of Nations,

"because the clergy—Catholic and Protestant —claiming to be God's representatives, have abandoned his plan and endorsed the League of Nations, hailing it as a political expression of Christ's kingdom on earth."*

The League of Nations came into being in 1919 and began really to function when it was ratified by the signatory powers at Paris on January 10, 1920. But Jehovah's servants continued to proclaim the Messianic kingdom of God. When the ban on *The Finished Mystery* was lifted, they resumed its circulation and, with it as a textbook, they continued to study the book of Ezekiel. As time went on and further developments fulfilled the prophecy of Ezekiel, a three-volume set of books titled "Vindication" provided an up-to-date understanding, showing more fully the application of the prophecy.

Thus this group of anointed followers of Jesus Christ, doing a work in Christendom paralleling Ezekiel's work among the

* See the *Federal Council Bulletin,* Volume II, No. 1, of the year 1919, pages 12-14.

Jews, were manifestly the modern-day Ezekiel, the "prophet" commissioned by Jehovah to declare the good news of God's Messianic kingdom and to give warning to Christendom. It is significant that, in 1931, after twelve years of faithful service despite the opposition of Christendom's clergy, these followers of Christ embraced the name "Jehovah's witnesses" at the same convention at which the book *Vindication* was released.—Isa. 43:10-12, *American Standard Version.*

PROPHET SENT TO "REBELLIOUS NATIONS"

When Jehovah spoke to the Jewish priest Ezekiel, commissioning him as his prophet, he said: "Son of man, I am sending you to the sons of Israel, to rebellious nations that have rebelled against me." (Ezek. 2:3) Who are those who constitute the "sons of Israel" and the "rebellious nations" against Jehovah, in this "time of the end"?

Back there in Ezekiel's day the Israelite people to whom Ezekiel was sent could be called "rebellious nations" because in 997 B.C.E. ten of the tribes of Israel had revolted against rule by the royal line of David, who sat on "Jehovah's throne." (1 Chron. 29:23) Thus there came to be two kingdoms or "nations." The Kingdom of Israel set up golden calves for worship and the Kingdom of Judah later also rebelled against Jehovah by breaking his laws and engaging in idolatry.

In the modern fulfillment, who are the "rebellious nations" that have rebelled against Jehovah? Their counterpart is Christendom. The Bible gives the proof. For Christendom has applied to herself the apostle Paul's words at Galatians 6:15, 16 (*Authorized Version*): "For in Christ Jesus neither circumcision availeth any thing, nor uncircumcision, but a new creature. And as many as walk according to this rule, peace be on them, and mercy,

and upon the Israel of God." For instance, in his "A Commentary and Critical Notes" (1836 edition), the Wesleyan Methodist minister Dr. Adam Clarke makes this comment on the expression "The Israel of God": "The *true Christians,* called here the *Israel of God,* to distinguish them from *Israel according to the flesh.*"

Romans 2:29 (*AV*) corroborates the above understanding. The apostle says: "But he is a Jew, which is one inwardly; and circumcision is that of the heart, in the spirit, and not in the letter; whose praise is not of men, but of God."

The history of Christendom shows that she has not been true to her claim of being "the Israel of God." From the fourth century on she has shown herself to be apostate, rebellious against Jehovah and his Word of truth. Corresponding to Israel's history, there was a break between the Greek churches and the Latin churches in 1054 C.E., when the Roman pope's legates excommunicated Patriarch Michael Cerularius of Constantinople.

Later, in 1529 C.E., the Protestant movement was established by the followers of ex-priest Martin Luther, and in 1534 the king of England, Henry VIII, was declared to be the Supreme Head of the Church of England. After this, numerous non-Roman Catholic sects sprang up, so that a number of so-called "Christian" lands have their own national State churches. Therefore Christendom can be called "nations," and their attitude toward God's Word the Bible and toward his Messianic kingdom is one of rebellion toward Jehovah. They continue to prefer political man-rule.

JEHOVAH'S "PROPHET" VINDICATED

Ezekiel's name meant "God Strengthens," and in order to carry out his mission to the end he needed God's help, for the professed people of God to whom he was sent were "insolent of face and hard of heart." At the time, they might not view or appreciate him as a prophet of Jehovah. Nevertheless, whether they paid attention to him or refrained, the occasion was to come when these rebellious people would "know also that a prophet himself happened to be in the midst of them." Jehovah would confirm him as a prophet then by causing what Ezekiel prophesied to come true. (Ezek. 2:3-5) Ezekiel was further told:

"And you, O son of man, do not be afraid of them; and of their words do not be afraid, because there are obstinate ones and things pricking you and it is among scorpions that you are dwelling. Of their words do not you be afraid, and at their faces do not you be struck with terror, for they are a rebellious house. And you must speak my words to them, regardless of whether they hear or they refrain, for they are a case of rebellion." —Ezek. 2:6, 7.

Since the year 1919 C.E. Jehovah's witnesses have found circumstances to be just like that as they have made the widest possible declaration of the good news of the Kingdom in 207 lands of the earth.

To Ezekiel, in his vision, and, symbolically to the modern-day "prophet," the spirit-begotten, anointed ones who are the nucleus of Jehovah's witnesses today, God gave something to eat. Ezekiel says:

"And I began to see ... a hand ... there w ... ually sp ... written ... there we ... ges and moaning and wailing."—Ezek. 2:8-10.

No space on the scroll being wasted, it being written upon on both sides, it was a full message, containing a great deal of gloomy messages of calamity, back there to Jewry, and today to Christendom. Why so? Because in both instances Jehovah's professed people were so rebellious and set in their ungodly way that Jehovah had to pronounce judgment upon them.

The scroll was doubtless delivered to Ezekiel by the hand of one of the cherubs in the vision. This would indicate that Jehovah's witnesses today make their declaration of the good news of the Kingdom under angelic direction and support. (Rev. 14:6, 7; Matt. 25:31, 32) And since no word or work of Jehovah can fail, for he is God Almighty, the nations will see the fulfillment of what these witnesses say as directed from heaven.

Yes, the time must come shortly that the nations will have to know that really a "prophet" of Jehovah was among them. Actually now more than a million and a half persons are helping that collective or composite "prophet" in his preaching work and well over that number of others are studying the Bible with the "prophet" group and its companions.

So Jehovah has made every provision for individuals to know him and to receive his loving-kindness and life. Thus there is no excuse for Christendom's people not to know Jehovah. More than that, Jehovah is interested not only in the vindication of his own name but also in vindicating his "prophet." Through another of his ancient prophets, Isaiah, he said to Jewry just as he says to Christendom today: "Look! My own ser... ully be... heart, ... ies be... ou will ... breakdown of spirit."—Isa. 65:14.

How do Jehovah's Witnesses make their declaration of the good news of the Kingdom?

Even today we hear complaints from Christendom's churches about dwindling church attendance and see many young men abandoning the priesthood and the ministerial profession. Yet at the same time we see spiritual prosperity and contentment among those proclaiming Jehovah's Messianic kingdom. We may look for an even more marked fulfillment of Isaiah's words in the near future.

With what do the pages of the Watchtower gleam?

Not Published in Any Books

TOO many and too rapid now are those unfoldings of Bible prophecy and truths, so that books cannot be written and published fast enough by the Watch Tower Society to present them all. But

YOU CAN GET THEM in that only magazine of its kind:

The Watchtower

No commercial ads of any kind take up any of its valuable space, nor does it engage in controversies over the politics, economics and religion of this world.

THIS MAGAZINE stands only for Jehovah God and his Government by Christ Jesus. Its pages gleam with the Scriptural and prophetic truths now due to be published for the education, comfort and guidance of all who now desire to take their stand (and hold it) on the side of God and his Son, Earth's Rightful Ruler.

Issued twice a month, each issue 16 pages, with the regular contributions from the pen of Judge Rutherford, international authority on Bible and government questions. Subscription price: $1.00 a year; for foreign countries, $1.50. For "terms to the Lord's poor" write the publishers. Send your subscription to

THE WATCH TOWER
117 Adams St., Brooklyn, N. Y., U. S. A.

3. THE WATCHTOWER AND PROPHECY

Since the Watchtower claims to be Jehovah's prophet who speaks in His name under angelic direction to warn us of the future, the biblical test of a prophet stipulated by Moses and Jesus must be applied to this modern-day prophet.

The following pages contain questions and official Watchtower literature from which the questions can be answered. The reader can answer the questions by studying the Watchtower literature. He can then see what prophecies have been given by the Watchtower.

ZION'S WATCH AND TOWER

HERALD OF CHRIST'S PRESENCE.

"Watchman, What of the Night?" "The Morning Cometh."—Isaiah xxi. 11.

VOL. VII   PITTSBURGH, PA., JANUARY, 1886   No. 5

VIEW FROM THE TOWER

The outlook at the opening of the New Year has some very encouraging features. The outward evidences are that the marshalling of the hosts for the battle of the great day of God Almighty, is in progress, while the skirmishing is commencing. While the Protestant (?) sects are coming daily into closer sympathy with the "Mother Church," as they rightly call the Church of Rome, the governments are ⌐ likewise. The latest proof of this is found :- January 1, 1886, in which i⸺ government, whi⸺ with.''

When would the time come for the Messiah to overthrow all earthly powers and establish His kingdom on earth?

⸺ which is richly set in ⸺ was accompanied by an autograph ⸺ rope, and in return Emperor William of Prussia has decorated the Pope's chief secretary, Cardinal Jacobini, with the "Order of the Black Eagle," the most honorable decoration of the Prussians.

of earth's kingdoms;* because the *time* is come for Messiah to take the dominion of earth and to overthrow the oppressors and corrupters of the earth, (Rev. 19:15 and 11:17, 18.) preparatory to the establishment of everlasting peace upon the only firm foundation of righteousness and truth.

Meantime, while those who are in opposition to the kingdom of God and its scepter of righteousness, impartiality and ⸺ce, are being gathered to the great slaughter referred to ⸺², (See Luke 19:27.) the Lord's professed Church is having ⸺ts trial completed. Its testing "so as by fire" is being ⸺plished, and the stewards are being heard as to the ⸺ulness or slothfulness of their stewardship. (Luke ⸺:15.) We see and *feel* this daily also, another evidence that the time for the glorifying of the Church the body of Christ, is nigh at hand, after which they will shortly be manifested for the joy and blessing of the groaning creation. Rom. 8:19-23.

From the TOWER is seems evident that the deeply interested are daily becoming more so, as inspired by the truth they

What of this you ask? A fulfilling of prophecy we reply. In the battle already beginning, we are clearly told that there will be a general division of the world into two contending parties. The kings, chief men, and mighty or influential men, the wealthy and the worldly great, are all on one side the battle, and with them the symbolic beast (Papacy) and Protestantism. All these unite their efforts, realizing that they must stand or fall together. (Rev. 19:18-20.) On the other side is the now present Lord, who, having taken his great power, begins the work of blessing the world by smiting down the oppressors—oppressive errors, and those influenced by the favors of those oppressive errors, who attempt to monopolize the favors of God both temporal and spiritual, and to oppress the people in their own advancement.

But who are with the Lord in this great work of smiting down error and oppression? The kings of earth? No. Financiers and capitalists? No; their interests are on the other side the question also. And where will the professed ministers of Christ stand who were sent to declare the good tidings of the deliverance which the King of kings is now bringing about? Where will the dignitaries and the influence of the Nominal Church be found? With the Lord? Ah, no; they have become so identified with the world that their interests will be bound up together, and their influence will be given on the side of error and oppression, on the side of kings and capitalists from whom they receive their support and upon whom they have become dependent.

Who then are with the King of kings in this conflict? Those close to him, his "regular army," are few—a little flock. Among these his followers, all faithful and true, are not many great, or rich, or mighty, according to the course of this world; but they are all rich in faith—chosen and faithful. (Rev. 17:14.) But the new and rightful King has an immense army of "irregulars" in every kind of uniform (except the white of the "regulars") Communists, Infidels, Socialists, Anarchists, Nihilists; all these fight in the battle of the great day, though ignorant of him whose kingdom they help to establish. These are the vultures of Rev. 19:17, 18, 21, who battle for plunder and get their fill in the overturning

are making effort at the cost of inconvenience and sacrifices of various kinds to spread the glad tidings; while others who love the present world and its honors and comforts are becoming more and more cold and indifferent. This, too, is what we should expect. We are in the testing-time, and must take our stand on one side or the other.

Many who inquired for the "suggestions" offered in our issue of September last, and engaged more actively in the work, are finding it a favorable opportunity for reaching hearing ears; and more than that we notice that their own hearts are being enkindled with the flame of the heavenly love in the message which they bear to those who sit in gross darkness all around them.

All this is encouraging, and in the name of the Master, we bid his faithful ones be of good cheer, and of thankful heart; while we trust that we all shall be more faithful and more used in the blessed service during the year begun, and that it shall be yet more rich in grace, knowledge, love, and good works, of faithful stewardship, let us render thanks for the favors and blessings past; for by the grace of God we are what and where we are.

To all the readers of the TOWER the Editor sends greeting and best wishes for the year 1886. May it be to all of you "A Happy New Year," Happy may ye be because of God's favors, realizing them in all the affairs of life, especially in the increasing knowledge of His plan and word of truth; in the privilege of suffering reproach and dishonor for the truth's sake, rejoicing and being exceeding glad that He counts you worthy, to thus share the sufferings of Christ. (Acts 5:41.) May you have abundant and well improved opportunity for suffering reproach for the name of Christ and in suffering for well doing. (1 Pet. 4:14-16.) And being thus proved worthy of the everlasting glory reserved in heaven for such as thus follow in the Master's footsteps, may you have at the same time the joy of the Lord, rejoicing with an unwavering hope in "the glory that shall be revealed in us." Rom. 8:18.

---

* [This view of the physical aspects of the conflict is not out of harmony with the explanation offered in Volume VII of Scripture Studies, which treats the subject from the symbolical standpoint.]

obtained the dominion (Dan. 2: 37, 38) ; Medo-Persia existed before it conquered Babylon ; and so with all ? ?
they must first have existed ?? ? ?
power before ?? ?

When will "the battle of God Almighty" end?
What was to happen to earth's rulership in 1915?

?? ?or
?? ?iu at large, was
?? ??rs that be," " ordained of God."
??cir "seven times" shall end, the Kingdom of God
cannot come into universal dominion. However, like the
others, it must obtain power adequate to the overthrow of
these kingdoms before it shall break them in pieces.

So, in this " Day of Jehovah," the " Day of Trouble,"
our Lord takes his great power (hitherto dormant) and reigns,
and this it is that will cause the trouble, though the world
will not so recognize it for some time. That the saints
shall share in this work of breaking to pieces present kingdoms, there can be no doubt. It is written, " This honor
have all his saints—to execute the judgments written, to
bind their kings with chains, and their nobles with fetters
of iron "—of strength. (Psa. 149 : 8, 9.) "He that over-
cometh, and keepeth my works unto the end, to him will I
give power over the nations, and he shall rule them with a
rod of iron ; as the vessels of a potter shall they [the *empires*]
be broken to shivers."—Rev. 2 : 26, 27 ; Psa. 2 : 8, 9.

But our examination, in the preceding volume, of the great
difference in character between the Kingdom of God and
the beastly kingdoms of earth, prepares us to see also a
difference in modes of warfare. The methods of conquest
and breaking will be widely different from any which have
ever before overthrown nations. He who now takes his
great power to reign is shown in symbol (Rev. 19:15) as
the one whose sword went forth *out of his mouth*, "that with
it he should smite the nations; and he shall rule them with
a rod of iron." That sword is the TRUTH (Eph. 6 : 17);

and the living saints, as well as many of the world, are now being used as the Lord's soldiers in overthrowing errors and evils. But let no one hastily infer a *peaceable conversion* of the nations to be here symbolized; for many scriptures, Such as Rev. 11:17, 18; Dan. 12:1; 2 Thes. 2:8; Psalms 149 and 47, teach the very opposite.

Be not surprised, then, when in subsequent chapters we present proofs that the setting up of the Kingdom of God is already begun, that it is pointed out in prophecy as due to begin the exercise of power in A. D. 1878, and that the "battle of the great day of God Almighty" (Rev. 16:14.), which will end in A.D. 1915, with the complete overthrow of earth's present rulership, is already commenced. The gathering of the armies is plainly visible from the standpoint of God's Word.

If our vision be unobstructed by prejudice, when we get the telescope of God's Word rightly adjusted we may see with clearness the character of many of the events due to take place in the "Day of the Lord"—that we are in the very midst of those events, and that "the Great Day of His Wrath is come."

The sword of truth, already sharpened, is to smite every evil system and custom—civil, social and ecclesiastical. Nay, more, we can see that the smiting is commenced: freedom of thought, and human rights, civil and religious, long lost sight of under kings and emperors, popes, synods, councils, traditions and creeds, are being appreciated and asserted as never before. The internal conflict is already fomenting: it will ere long break forth as a consuming fire, and human systems, and errors, which for centuries have fettered truth and oppressed the groaning creation, must melt before it. Yes, truth—and widespread and increasing knowledge of it—is the sword which is perplexing and wounding the heads over many countries. (Psa. 110:6.)

Thirdly, the present government and emperor are very popular. The last ten years have witnessed for the masses a great social and financial elevation; laws have been enacted for the protection, and gradually for the betterment, of the poorer classes; and the present emperor has very wisely addressed himself to various liberal reforms for their amelioration.

Our judgment therefore is that, so long as these conditions prevail, Germany can control the anarchistic or lawless elements within her borders, and is not likely to experience a social revolution for some years to come.

Germany's military preparation is so well known to the leading statesmen of Europe that no nation is likely to seek a quarrel with her; and her strain to keep up her present standard is so great that she wants no increase of it such as war would bring. Hence, with Austria and Italy in league and largely in the same plight and under her influence, Germany is today, humanly speaking, the arbiter of the world's peace.

Furthermore, we found that throughout ...

Indeed, the houses oc ... southern Russia, comp ... similar class in this c ... in Pittsburgh which ar ... tenements observed on ...

> **What date is set for the close of "that battle"?
> From what date do we mark its beginning?**

... not even excepting the slums of London, Liverpool, Edinburgh and Glasgow, which are the worst we saw in Europe, Russia alone excepted.

The people are generally intelligent, industrious, busy and comfortably clothed and fed—far beyond our previous suppositions. We could not help wondering whence come some of the worst specimens of all races to this country as emigrants. Evidently the people of the United States are performing a service of inestimable value to the whole world in receiving their scum of ignorance and their dregs of degradation—both due more to evils of the past than to those of the present, and chiefly chargeable to priestcraft, superstition and ignorance fostered for centuries by our that old "Mother of Harlots," which falsely claims to be the church-system founded by our Lord and his apostles. The wonder often is that, with almost no assistance except the necessity and opportunity for industry, so many of these degraded members of the human family

the people to feel that they have nothing to lose, but all to gain, by a general uprising.

While it was an agreeable surprise to us (in view of the contrary sensational accounts so often published) to find the situation in Europe as we here describe it—in harmony with what the Scriptures had led us to expect—yet so great is our confidence in the Word of God and in the light of present truth shining upon it, that we could not have doubted its testimony whatever had been the appearances. The date of the close of that "battle" is definitely marked in Scripture as October, 1914. It is already in progress, its beginning dating from October, 1874. Thus far it has been chiefly a battle of words and a time of organizing forces—capital, labor, armies and secret societies.

Never was there such a general time of banding together as at present. Not only ... ations allying with each other for protection ... tions, but the various factions in ... to protect their several interests ... factions are merely studying ... gth of their opponents, and ...l power for the future struggle ... the Bible's testimony, seem to realize ... Others still delude themselves, saying, ...evitable. ...reace! Peace! when there is no possibility of peace until God's kingdom comes into control, compelling the doing of his will on earth as it is now done in heaven.

This feature of the battle must continue with varying success to all concerned; the organization must be very thorough; and the final struggle will be comparatively short, terrible and decisive—resulting in general anarchy. In many respects the convictions of the world's great generals coincide with the predictions of God's Word. Then "Woe to the man or nation who starts the next war in Europe; for it will be a war of *extermination*." It will be abetted not only by national animosities, but also by social grievances, ambitions and amimosities, and if not brought to an end by the establishment of God's kingdom in the hands of his elect and then glorified Church, it would exterminate the race.—Matt. 24:22.

THE CHURCH'S SHARE IN THE BATTLE

The Scriptures show also that the battle of the great day will begin with the church of God, and that the overthrow of the great nominal church systems will precede the overthrow of the present civil powers; for the Lord is about to shake, not only the earth (the civil organization of society) but heaven (the ecclesiastical powers) also (Heb. 12:26), to the end that great "Babylon," falsely called Christendom—Christ's kingdom—may be completely destroyed. The great counterfeit kingdom of Christ, with all its allied civil and ecclesiastical powers, must go down as a great millstone into the sea, preparatory to the final establishment of the true kingdom of Christ. Here, as in the world at large, the work of preparation is going on. The creeds, which for years have been reverenced and received without questioning, are now called up for inspection; and their inconsistencies and lack of Bible foundation is being discovered. As a consequence, the clergy, whose living and honors and worldly prospects in general are all bound up with the systems held together by these creeds, are in great trouble, and are looking about to see what can be done to strengthen the stakes and lengthen the cords of so-called Christianity. A general union of the various sects is suggested, with a simple creed formulated from the various points of agreement among them all and the ignoring of all other points of doctrine to which objection might be made by some.

This scheme meets with very general approval from all the sects, and the trend of their efforts is in this direction. This, too, is in harmony with prophecy, which shows, not only that the various sects of "Protestantism" will band together as one, but that there will also be a close affiliation with Roman Catholicism. These two ends of the ecclesiastical heaven will roll together as a scroll (Isa. 34:4), the two rolls, Protestantism and Romanism, coming closer and closer together as their power over the masses of the people decreases.

This work is already progressing very rapidly: church congresses for the consideration of various schemes of union are the order of the day. All the various branches of Presbyterianism are considering the feasibility of union: so also of Methodism, Congregationalism, and others. When each of these is consolidated, their respective denominations will have a greater prestige in the world; and when all Protestant sects are more firmly united under some one name, such as "The Evangelical Alliance," the prestige of Protestantism as a whole will be greatly augmented, though we think the term Protestantism will probably be dropped entirely as a concession to the church of Rome, to secure its favor. Such an organiza-

turn out as favorably as they do. What a field here at our door for mission workers, evangelists and philanthropists—if they but realized it, than any foreign mission field we saw. And these emigrants, let us remember, although generally poor, are not always either ignorant or vicious. Some of them are God's consecrated saints whom he is sending here to be blessed and sealed with present truth, which he gives us the privilege of ministering to them.

True, the food of the lower classes of Europe would not be satisfactory to the average mechanic and laborer in the United States, who, accustomed to larger pay and unaccustomed to frugality, spends probably six times as much on his stomach, eating not only finer and more nutritious foods, but also much more of them, and wasting often through improvidence as much as or more than he eats. However, the European laborer seems to enjoy himself as much as or more than his artisan brother here, and on the whole there is more of an appearance of contentment on the faces of all the people there—the poor, the middle class and the rich—than on faces met in the streets here.

Intelligence without the grace of God to back it up brings discontent: only when it is backed by godliness, does it bring contentment, peace and joy. For this reason it is that the greater general intelligence and greater liberty of the people of the United States bring them, not more contentment, but less than their less favorably circumstanced European brothers. And this leads us to expect as stirring times in the United States as elsewhere when the "time of trouble" shall reach its height.

While the growing intelligence of Europeans is fast preparing them for the trouble and anarchy which God's Word predicts, it cannot reasonably be expected for some years yet. This is further in harmony with prophecy, though out of harmony with the expectations of many who look every day for a declaration of war in Europe, which they suppose will be the *battle of the great day of God Almighty*. Even should a war or revolution break out in Europe sooner than 1905, we could not consider it any portion of the severe trouble predicted. At most it could only be a forerunner to it, a mere "skirmish" as compared with what is to come. Indeed, in our judgment, based upon our observations, nothing could precipitate the great anarchistic trouble upon Europe, which the Scriptures predict, sooner than the date named, except a *famine* or some such unusual occurrence which would bring

That the earthly phase of the Kingdom will be on terms
of intimate communion, fellowship and coöperation with
the Kingdom proper, the spiritual rulers, is evident. They
will be related to each oth~

What phase of the kingdom is about to be set up?
We are in the end of what age?
What does Oct. 1874 signify?
What does April 1878 mean in terms of the kingdom?

.... [the divine messages, through the "princes"] from
Jerusalem."—Isa. 2:3.

SETTING UP THE KINGDOM.

"The Kingdom of God is preached, and every man
[accepting the testimony as a message from God] presseth
into it." (Luke 16:16.) For over eighteen centuries this
message, this offer of the Kingdom, has been doing its in-
tended work of selecting the "elect" "overcomers" from
the world. During all this age these have waited the Father's
time for their *setting up* or exaltation to power, as his Kings
and priests, to rule and to teach the redeemed people of
the earth, and thus bring to them the opportunity of everlasting life through faith and obedience. Yet during all
this time this Kingdom class has suffered violence at the
hands of the Ishmael and Esau class, and at the hands
of Satan, the prince of this world, and his blinded servants. As our Lord expressed it,—"The Kingdom of Heaven
suffereth violence, and the violent take it by force." (Matt.
11:12.) Our Lord, the head of the Kingdom, suffered to
the extent of death; and all of his followers have suffered
something of earthly loss as a consequence of being trans-

lated out of the power of darkness into the Kingdom of God's dear Son.—Col. 1:13.

This *submission* for over eighteen centuries to the violence of dominant evil has not been because of lack of power on the part of our risen, ascended and glorified Lord to protect his people; for after his resurrection he declared,— "All power is given unto me in heaven and in earth." (Matt. 28:18.) The exercise of the power is delayed for a purpose. In the Father's plan there was a "due time" for the great sacrifice for sins to be given, and another due time for the Kingdom to be set up in power and great glory to rule and bless the world: and these were far enough apart to permit the calling and preparing of the "elect" Church to be joint-heirs of the Kingdom with Christ. The evil influences and opposition of sinners have been *permitted* for the purifying, testing and polishing of those "called" to be members of the Kingdom class. As with the Head, so with the body, it is God's design that each member shall as a new creature be "made perfect through suffering."— Heb. 5:9.

But now we are in the end of this Gospel age, and the Kingdom is being established or set up. Our Lord, the appointed King, is now present, since October 1874, A. D., according to the testimony of the prophets, to those who have ears to hear it; and the formal inauguration of his kingly office dates from April 1878, A. D. : and the first work of the Kingdom, as shown by our Lord, in his parables and prophecy (the gathering of "his elect"), is now in progress. "The dead in Christ shall rise *first*," explained the Lord through the Apostle; and the resurrection of the Church shall be in a moment.* Consequently the Kingdom, as represented in our Lord, and the sleeping saints already fitted and prepared and found worthy to be members of

---

* VOL III. Chap. 6.

against going to an extreme in the contrary direction. The thought of the Scriptures on the subject is expressed again in the Apostle's words, "Provide things honest in the sight of all men;" and again, "He that provideth not for his own . . . hath denied the faith and is worse than an unbeliever."—Rom. 12: 17; 1 Tim. 5: 8.

The thought would appear to be that every parent owes it to his child to give him more of a start in life than merely the imperfect dying little body born into the world. Having brought children into the world, it becomes the duty of parents to see to their reasonable and proper establishment in it. This includes not only the dispensing of food and raiment during childhood and youth, but also the provision of intellectual and moral instructions to which we have already referred; and all this means laying up, laying aside from personal consumption, in the interest of the children. Seeing the uncertainties of life, it would not be an unreasonable application of the Scriptural injunction for the parent to have something laid up for the necessities of his family in the event of his death before they had reached maturity. It is not our thought that the Apostle meant that parents should seek to lay up fortunes for their children to quarrel over and to be injured by. The child fairly well born and who receives a reasonable education and guidance to maturity, is well off, has a rich legacy in himself; and the parent who has made such provision for his children has every reason to feel that he has been ruled in the matter by the sound mind, the holy Spirit, the right disposition, approved by the Lord, even though he leave no property to his family, or not more than a shelter or home. Such a man has discharged his stewardship and such children will be sure in the end to appreciate his faithfulness.

ORGANIZATIONS FOR MUTUAL BENEFIT, ETC.

We are living in a day of organization, and it must be admitted that some of these have been and are truly wise and beneficial arrangements. Insurance companies of every kind are, of course, on a commercial

footing, not, strictly speaking, philanthropic. They are
endeavors on the part of humanity to bridge over the
uncertainties and difficulties of the present li⸱⸱
provision ahead for death an⸱⸱ ⸱⸱
the affairs of ⸱⸱⸱

> **What date signals the end of "the times
> of the Gentiles"?**
>
> **When would "the stress of the great time of trouble"
> take place?**

⸱⸱⸱lves

⸱⸱⸱cumstances in which we consider
⸱⸱⸱ lather of a family did wisely in keeping an
insurance policy for the benefit of his wife and children.
Especially is this a wise course where the wife is not in
sympathy with Present Truth and the husband's views
respecting the near future, and when she desires insurance as a protection and as a rest and relief to her
mind. If the husband's judgment in any considerable
degree coincides with that of his wife, we think he would
do well to maintain such insurance. We are not ad-
vocating insurance, and as for the writer, he carries
none. We are merely pointing out that nothing in the
Scriptures is designed to govern or regulate the conduct
of New Creatures in this respect, and that each must
use his own judgment in harmony with his own peculiar conditions in deciding the matter.

<u>According to our expectations the stress of the great
time of trouble will be on us soon, somewhere between
1910 and 1912—culminating with the end of the "Times
of the Gentiles," October, 1914.</u>*

The beginning of the severity of the trouble is not distinctly marked in the Scriptures, and is rather conjectural.
We infer that so great a trouble, so world-wide a catas-
trophe, could scarcely be accomplished in less than three
years, and that if it lasted much more than three years
"no flesh would be saved." In harmony with these
anticipations we expect that when the financial storm
shall sweep over Christendom, business and banks and
insurance and property values will all go down together;

*See Vol. II., pp. 76-78. Accordingly the culmination of the fostering
forces came in the Autumn of 1914 with the outbreak of the great European
war—a stage in the overthrow of Satan's Empire.

STUDIES

IN THE

SCRIPT

> Before what date will the last member of the church be glorified?
> What date will see the conversion of the Jews?

SERIES II

The Time is at Hand

1,154,000 Edition.

"Times of Refreshing Shall Come From the Presence of the Lord; and He Shall Send Jesus Christ, * * * Whom the Heavens Must Retain until

THE TIMES OF RESTITU-
TION OF ALL THINGS

Which God Hath Spoken by the Mouth of All His Holy Prophets Since the World Began." "Ye Brethren, Are Not in Darkness, That That Day Should Overtake You as a Thief."—Acts 3: 19-21; 1 Thes. 5: 4.

INTERNATIONAL BIBLE STUDENTS ASSOCIATION
BROOKLYN, LONDON, MELBOURNE, BARMEN,
ELBERFELD, OREBRO, CHRISTIANIA.

1912

In this chapter we present the Bible evidence proving that the full end of the times of the Gentiles, *i. e.*, the full end of their lease of dominion, will be reached in A. D.

1914; and that that date will be the farthest limit of the rule of imperfect men. And be it observed, that if this is shown to be a fact firmly established by the Scriptures, it will prove:—

Firstly, That at that date the Kingdom of God, for which our Lord taught us to pray, saying, "Thy Kingdom come," will obtain full, universal control, and that it will then be "set up," or firmly established, in the earth, on the ruins of present institutions.

Secondly, It will prove that he whose right it is thus to take the dominion will then be present as earth's new Ruler; and not only so, but it will also prove that he will be present for a considerable period before that date; because the overthrow of these Gentile governments is directly caused by his dashing them to pieces as a potter's vessel (Psa. 2:9; Rev. 2:27), and establishing in their stead his own righteous government.

Thirdly, It will prove that some time before the end of A. D. 1914 the last member of the divinely recognized Church of Christ, the "royal priesthood," "the body of Christ," will be glorified with the Head; because every member is to reign with Christ, being a joint-heir with him of the Kingdom, and it cannot be fully "set up" without every member.

Fourthly, It will prove that from that time forward Jerusalem shall no longer be trodden down of the Gentiles, but shall arise from the dust of divine disfavor, to honor; because the "Times of the Gentiles" will be fulfilled or completed.

Fifthly, It will prove that by that date, or sooner, Israel's blindness will begin to be turned away; because their "blindness in part" was to continue only "*until* the fulness of the Gentiles be come in" (Rom. 11:25), or, in other words, until the full number from among the Gentiles, who are to be members of the body or bride of Christ, would be fully selected.

Sixthly, It will prove that the great "time of trouble such

THE WATCH TOWER

and angry with the kings, rulers, nobles, will result in the anarchy which will doubtless prevail throughout Europe—and extend to every nation, as the Bible predicts. We understand that Christ's kingdom is associated with this in the sense that Christ is about to take to himself his great power and reign. The Lord speaks of the anarchists as "his great army," in a figurative way, just as he speaks of the caterpillars, which are used figuratively to represent his army. The saints will not be in that army at all. The Lord has used even the devil as his agent, and "the wrath of man to praise him." Anarchists may be part of the Lord's great army in that he will supervise their campaign.

Eventually, the United States will become involved, and so fall with the other nations; not necessarily because the United States will engage in this war, however. To do so would be very foolish indeed. Our government is strong enough people govern themselves; they have their own ___ and their own liberties, and can chan___ believe that they are doing ___ paring to do so still further ___ will come down to a sociali___ happen, the wealthy, seeking t___ _ themselves, will doubtless bring things to pass in violation of the laws, and will thus precipitate trouble, believing that they are resisting injustice. Wise would it be for all to accept as gracefully as possible the inevitable leveling; but will they be wise?

It is human nature to make the streets run with blood rather than to suffer defeat and surrender "vested rights." The people are being led on by hatred, and an appeal to unreason. While certain truths are presented, the presentation is not truthful. But many are being inoculated, and are pre-

paring, as they think, for Socialism—we would say, for anarchism, here as easily as in Europe.

ARMAGEDDON STILL FUTURE

While it is possible that Armageddon may begin next Spring, yet it is purely speculation to attempt to say just when. We see, however, that there are parallels between the close of the Jewish age and this Gospel age. These parallels seem to point to the year just before us—particularly the early months.

The Scriptures indicate that the Gentile governments will receive from their own peoples their first notice that their lease of power has expired ___ ple will take note of the sign of the Son o___ ens. The judgments of the Lord ___ the world, and will run ___ this manifestation of his ___ ___ the epiphania, the shining forth, ___, or the King of Glory. "He shall be re-___ __ in flaming fire, taking vengeance on them that know not God, and that obey not the Gospel of our Lord Jesus Christ." (2 Thessalonians 1:7-10) As a result, the nations of earth will be broken to pieces like a potter's vessel.—Psalm 2:8, 9.

The prophetic forecast tells us that the trouble will begin in the ecclesiastical heavens, and later will proceed to the social element. The picture given of the end of Gentile times is that of a stone striking the image of Gentile supremacy in its feet. (Daniel 2:34, 35) The impact will be so sharp and so thorough as to leave nothing of them. Having had their day, they will cease to be—"become like the chaff of the summer threshing floor." The next event in order will be the Messianic kingdom, of which it is written, "The desire of all peoples shall come."

| What date for Armageddon seems to be indicated? |

"MAN PROPOSES—GOD DISPOSES"

[Reprint from our issue of October 15, 1898, which please see.]

THE TRIED AND PROVEN PEOPLE

"The Lord your God proveth you, to know whether ye love the Lord your God with all your heart and with all your soul."—Deut. 13:3.

"The Lord your God entered into a covenant with the Children of Is-

mandments or no. He humbled thee, and suffered thee to hun-

God had entered into a covenant with the Children of Is-

What battle was prophesied to follow World War I?
When will the kingdom be established on earth?
What date is assigned as the close of 6,000 years since Adam's creation?
What date is set for the 1,000-year reign of Christ?

"Distress of Nations With Perplexity"

Pastor Russell Says He Cannot Pray the Almighty to Change His Program--Tells Why Present War Will Proceed and Eventuate in No Glorious Victory for Either Side, But in the Horrible Mutilation and Impoverishment of All Nations.

PASTOR RUSSELL

Pastor Russell addressed a very intelligent audience last evening at the New York City Temple. His discourse was based on the text, "Upon the earth distress of nations with perplexity; the sea and the waves roaring; men's hearts failing them for fear and for looking after those things that are coming upon the earth." (Luke xxi., 25, 26.) He said:

Our Honorable President with praiseworthy intent has requested all Christian people to make this a day of prayer for peace in Europe. I have been asked to sermonize accordingly. However, I cannot concur with our worthy President in this matter. Much as I appreciate peace—and I have all my life labored to be a peacemaker—, cannot pray the Almighty to change His plans to conform to those of our honored President.

For 2,500 years God, through the Bible Prophets, has been telling His people about this great war and concerning the more terrible Armageddon which will follow it; and can we expect Him to reverse the programme at our behest?

The prayers of these millions praying for the prosperity of the Germans and the extermination of the Allies, and the prayers of other millions for the success of the Allies and the annihilation of the Germans, and the prayers of the Pope and of our President and other good people that this awful war shall promptly cease will all go unanswered, if I read my Bible aright. The war will proceed and will eventuate in no glorious victory for any nation, but in the horrible mutilation and impoverishment of all. Next will follow the Armageddon of anarchy.

After that, peace, lasting peace, may be hoped for, because God has declared it. It will be brought in by Messiah's Kingdom, for which so long we have prayed—"Thy Kingdom come!"

For forty years I have been proclaiming this very war and its glorious outcome by sermons, oral and printed, and in my books on Bible study in twenty languages. Now, when the very year has come and the prophecy is being fulfilled, could I consistently ask the Almighty to change His programme? Nay! Rather my discourse will be, as announced, from the Master's words respecting the present "distress of nations with perplexity, • • • men's hearts failing them for fear of those things about to come on the earth."

God's Part in the Present War.

Doubtless many will be shocked with my declaration that this war and the resulting greater calamity are of Divine other help than that which God Himself has provided.

From the creation of Adam until now has been a period of six thousand years—man's work week—during which he has been permitted to try everything he could imagine for his own relief from sin and its penalty of death.

So far from gaining life everlasting for our race, all our efforts have accomplished nothing. Our most learned physicians and specialists declare that the world is on the verge of collapse; and that at the present rate of increase there would not, in one hundred and sixty years, be enough sane people in the world to care for the insane. They tell us that various diseases are increasing so rapidly as to endanger the race in a very short time; and that this is so notwithstanding the fact that sanitary conditions are made necessary, even to the extent of individual drinking cups.

Our only hope lies in the great Seventh Day, the antitypical Sabbath. In it Messiah, associating with Himself the saintly ones of this Gospel Age, will set up the Divine Kingdom amongst men—a spiritual Kingdom, not an earthly one, but ruling amongst mankind, blessing and uplifting them. For a thousand years the work of uplift will proceed until all the willing and obedient will have attained again the lost likeness of their Creator; and the whole earth will be their Paradise.

"Times of the Gentiles."

Amongst other lessons which God has been teaching mankind is the fact that they are incapable of establishing a government such as is necessary for the real blessing and uplift of the race. God appointed Israel after the flesh to be His typical Kingdom for a time, and selected King David and his posterity to be rulers. By and by He cut these off, discontinuing the earthly typical Kingdom.

The last monarch of David's line was King Zedekiah, of whom we read: "O thou profane and wicked Prince, whose time has come that iniquity shall have an end. Remove the diadem, take off the crown. • • • I will overturn, overturn, overturn it until He comes whose right it is, and I will give it to Him." (Ezekiel xxi., 25-27.) Messiah is the One whose right it is—Jesus the Head, the Church His Body—on the spirit plane.

Certain Scriptures indicate that the period during which God's Kingdom would be removed would be seven prophetic Times, each 360 years long. Seven Times would therefore equal 2,520 years. Reckoned from the time of King Zedekiah, that period ends this year; for, according to the Scriptures, King Zedekiah's crown was taken away in 606 B. C. If so, with the close of the present year Messiah should take to Himself His great power and begin His glorious Reign of a thousand years, the beginning of which, according to the Bible, will be a very dark hour—"a Time of Trouble such as was not since there was a nation," "no, nor ever shall be " the like again.—Daniel, xii., 1; Matthew xxiv., 21.

...arger annual sums than ever before in interest. In case of failure the State will have to pass into the hands of the receiver, and in its ruin great commercial and financial hou... will be involved. We are all slaughterin... ...owers, and every week ... destruction.—

> ## To what was World War I supposed to lead?
> ## What was to happen right after World War I?

...nger. Austria-Hungary, again, is not a ... ...ike France. Suppose either Germany or Austria be... ...ome dismembered by external force, or exploded by revolu... ...tion, what becomes of their national or Imperial debts, or of the indemnities which the Allies might hope to exact! The ... ...here one looks into the financial and political future of Europe after the war the darker and more obscure do its problems appear. But that is all the more reason why inde... ...pendent men with knowledge and penetration and foresight ...ould exercise their minds upon the political economy of this war. Never has there been such a collision of forces, never so much destruction in so short a time. Never has it been so difficult or so necessary to measure the calamity, to count the costs, to foresee and provide against the consequences to human society. Philanthropists profess to hope that the peace settlement will bring with it a great international reduc... ...tion of armies and armaments, which will enable the nations to support their new war debt, and so to avoid the bankruptcy court. No doubt the fear of bankruptcy will count for ...something; otherwise the peace settlement might be expected to breed another series of preparations for another series of wars. But those who know the forces which really control the diplomacy of Europe see no Utopias. The outlook is for bloody revolutions and fierce wars between labor and capital, or between the masses and the governing classes of Continental Europe.

BIBLE STUDENTS AND THE FUTURE

In all the Continental armies our brethren, known as Bible Students, are to be found—not willingly, but by conscription. However opposed to the taking of life, they are subject to the powers that be in everything that does not conflict with conscience. Before the war we recommended to the brethren

Meantime, another danger to the Lord's consecrated people lies along the lines of worldly-mindedness—neglecting the kingdom in favor of the things of this present ... adversary is still alert. We, also, must be alert ...n of the light, children of the day, soldiers of the ...ere never was a better opportunity, than now for ...h the royal banner of our Redeemer. More people have ears to hear and sharper ears to hear than ever before. Thousands are anxious for the message which we have to give them and which they do not find elsewhere—the message of hope, the message which explains that the present reign of evil, and the past six thousand years of the reign of sin and death, have reached their culmination, and now they are about to be brought to an end by the great Redeemer, in fulfilment of our Heavenly Father's glorious plans which he purposed in himself from before the foundation of the world

SELL THE PHILIPPINES TO JAPAN

Two years ago, on our return from the Orient, we sent the below letter of suggestion to the Government with copies of it to the newspapers, some of which published the letter, which read as follows:—

Brooklyn, May 26, 1913.

Honorable Wm. J. Bryan, Secretary of State, U. S. A.

Dear Sir:—I am addressing you, and through you the Honorable President of this Nation, and the Honorable Members of its Congress, upon a subject which I believe to be of primo importance to our Nation and to the world. I would have preferred to make this communication a private one, but believe that its object will be much better served if it be known at home and abroad that the suggestion comes from a native citizen, a minister and ambassador of Christ, rather than if the same suggestion were to emanate from some Official of our Government or from a politician.

THE WORLD'S PEACE ENDANGERED

A year ago I visited Japan and observed the congested conditions there prevailing, and learned that her population is increasing very rapidly, while every foot of arable land is under "intense" cultivation. Japan's need for room for her overflow population has already led her to grasp Korea, and

[5659]

...at in the event of hostilities they should, so far as possible, if drafted, request positions in the hospital service or in the Government commissary department, where they could serve the Government decently; whereas, if they were ordered to the firing line, they would not be obliged to shoot to kill. We have reasons for believing that these suggestions are being followed and that meantime the brethren are using the opportunities for proclaiming to their companions in military service the blessed message of the soon-to-be-established kingdom of Christ, 'for the blessing of all the families of the earth.'

We have exhorted the brethren to strict neutrality so far as the combatants are concerned, whatever might be their natural inclination through accident of birth or association. To Bible Students none of the belligerent nations are wholly in the right, and none of them entirely to blame. Let us more and more seek to take the Bible view of the great Armageddon, of which we are now having the prelude. It is the outgrowth of our civilization, developing in the soil of selfishness. We are seeing fruits which have been ripening for forty years.

We are never for a moment to forget that if the nations were Christian nations, as some of us once supposed, they would be bearing the fruits of the Spirit—meekness, gentleness, patience, kindness, love. How great the mistake! Christendom—Christ's kingdom—has not yet been established. It awaits the Lord's time and the manifestation of his power and great glory in its establishment. These are kingdoms of this world, actuated by the principles of selfishness and deceived by Satan, "the god of this world."

The Battle of Armageddon, to which this war is leading, will be a great contest between right and wrong, and will signify the complete and everlasting overthrow of the wrong, and the permanent establishment of Messiah's righteous kingdom for the blessing of the world. All these things are probably easier to be seen from this side of the ocean than by the dear friends who are nearer to, and more directly influenced by, the war and their national, personal interests. Nevertheless, it is important that we all keep clearly before our minds that this is not the war of the church, but the war of the world with carnal weapons; and that our sympathies are broad enough to cover all engaged in the dreadful strife, as our hope is broad enough and deep enough to include all in the great blessings which our Master and his Millennial kingdom are about to bring to the world.

it is no secret that she longs for possession of the Philippine Islands, and would be glad of a reasonable pretext for taking possession of them. Many broad-minded Americans have suggested that the United States has no desire to acquire colonies in an imperial sense, and that, therefore, the Philippine Islands should be surrendered to the Filipinos. The only objection urged against this move is that the Filipinos are not as yet sufficiently advanced in civilization to properly govern themselves. And those most intimate with the situation have not the slightest doubt that if the United States withdrew from the Philippines, the Japanese Government would immediately take control, and shortly the Philippine Islands would be inundated with Japanese—undoubtedly much to their benefit, as the latter people are more thrifty, and prudent and energetic than the Filipinos.

SOME RADICAL SUGGESTIONS

I suggest that the United States Government select from amongst the Philippine Islands one island suitable as a naval base, and tender to Japan the opportunity to take over the Philippine Islands at precisely the same they have cost the United States. This would give our neighbors of the Far East exactly what they want, at no price at all compared with the cost of war. Additionally, it would make them our friends, and surely all Americans desire a world-wide friendship with all nations. I advise that this step be taken speedily, because there is a "jingo" party in Japan bent upon the acquirement of the Philippines, which party will always be ready to take advantage of such trifles as the California Alien Law to incite hatred against the United States and to force their Government, against its judgment, to seize the Philippines.

It is human nature for the Japanese to want those Islands—to feel that they need them. It is practical common sense to say that they can take them whenever they are ready. The United States could not retake the Philippines except at the expense of many lives and thousands of millions of dollars—if at all.

Our Japanese neighbors, flushed with their victory over the Russian Navy, and courageous and proud-spirited, anyway, realize fully their ability to capture the Philippines and probably to hold them; but they do not realize that a war with America would be a very different one from that with Russia—that American pride and valor would spend thou:

not close with A. D. 70, but progressed in various parts of the world thereafter. Quite a good ...... ing by their terrible experi... to be gathered into the Go of their national polity. Sir a good many will yet be gat ...... here. we know of no time-limit here.

Incidentally we remark that some historians put the end of the Jewish Time of Trouble as April A. D. 73, which would correspond to April 1918.

Are we regretful that the harvest work continues? Nay, verily; we rejoice and have the pleasure each day of showing forth the praises of him who hath called us out of darkness into his most marvelous light; and we delight in seeing how others are being benefited and made to rejoice. Are we regretful of the experiences we have had in coming to this present point? Do we feel like repining that the Lord did not force upon us more careful attention to the parallelism? Nay, verily; the Lord's leadings have been good. Perhaps, indeed, we got benefit from the thought that the harvest work would soon be ended. Perhaps it led us to deeper consecration and greater activity in the service of the Lord, in ourselves and for others. We therefore have nothing to regret.

"Who led us first, will lead us still,
Calmly we sink into His will."

THE BURNING OF THE TARES

In the parable of "the Wheat and the Tares," the Master puts very prominently the gathering of the tares and the binding of them in bundles for burning. We assumed that this burning would not take place until all the wheat had been gathered into the heavenly Garner; but apparently this was

> **When did the "Jewish Time of Trouble" end?**
> **What should "the eyes of understanding" discern?**

nering of the wheat continues; ... of the tares will correspond ... of Jordan. The tares are a who have risen up out of the ... aims of a benevolent character, ... From the ...... a peculiar ...... The

but misled into thinking that they are the church. From the tare viewpoint, the wheat are an abnormal growth, a peculiar people, few in number, and not held in high esteem. The smiting of the waters will reveal the truth in respect to what is the real church of Christ, and what are imitations; and the honest-minded tare class will be undeceived, and cease to longer pretend that they are the church of Christ—thus they will be burned or cease to be as tares, continuing however as noble-minded worldly people and will have a share in the general blessings of the "sweet by and by" under the kingdom, for which we still pray.

Our present attitude, dear brethren, should be one of great gratitude toward God, increasing appreciation of the beautiful truth which he has granted us the privilege of seeing and being identified with, and increasing zeal in helping to bring that truth to the knowledge of others. In the meantime, our eyes of understanding should discern clearly the Battle of the Great Day of God Almighty now in progress; and our faith, guiding our eyes of understanding through the Word, should enable us to see the glorious outcome—Messiah's kingdom.

Furthermore, we can be fully content not to know how long the harvest work will last—content that the great Captain, who by divine appointment has the entire matter in charge, is too wise to err, and has promised us that all of our experiences shall work together for our good if we love him and are of "the called ones according to his purpose," seeking to make our calling and election sure.

24:18. So I spake unto the people in the morning: and
at even my wife died; and I did in the morning as I was
commanded.—He continued his address~~
the Lord's people ~~

Until 1878, what was God's sanctuary or temple?
What date is now assigned as the end
of the churches?

~~   the~~
~~   falsehoods in connection with~~
~~this incident~~ of his life?

THE CHURCHES TO CEASE TO BE

24:20, 21. Then I answered them, The word of the Lord
came unto me, saying, Speak unto the house of Israel,
Thus saith the Lord God; Behold, I will profane My Sanctuary, the excellency of your strength, the desire of your
eyes, and that which your soul pitieth; and your sons and
your daughters whom ye have left shall fall by the sword.
—God gives the reason. It was as a picture or parable of
what is to happen to Christendom. Until 1878 the nominal
church had been in a sense God's sanctuary or Temple;
but He was from then on, culminating in 1918, to remove it
with a stroke or plague of erroneous doctrines and deeds
Divinely permitted. The Church was the strength of Christendom, that about which its life centered, and around
which its institutions were built. It was the desire of the
eyes of the people, that which all Christians loved. Nevertheless, God was to make manifest the profanation which
ecclesiasticism had made of the Christian Church, and to
cause the church organizations to become to Him as one
dead, an unclean thing, not to be touched, or mourned.
And the "children of the church" shall perish by the
sword of war, revolution and anarchy, and by the Sword
of the Spirit be made to see that they have lost their hope
of life on the spirit plane—that "the door is shut."
24:22. And ye shall do as I have done: ye shall not
cover your lips, nor eat the bread of men.—So universal
and dreadful will be the troubles that the dead will literally lie unburied and unwept. There can be no mourning
for the dead in a period when the living are overwhelmed
by troubles worse than death.
24:23. And your tires shall be upon your heads; and
your shoes upon your feet: ye shall not mourn nor weep;
but ye shall pine away for your iniquities, and mourn one
toward another.—The mourning will be an inner sorrow
of a people stupefied by terrible experiences, who pine

60

away and without outward expression sink together into the fellowship of helpless grief.

24:24. **Thus Ezekiel is unto you a sign: according to all that he hath done shall ye do: and when this cometh, ye shall know that I am the Lord God.**—Thus the silent sorrow at Pastor Russell's heart was to be a sign to Christendom. The sorrowful experiences of Pastor Russell in this connection shall later on be those of all Christendom; "and when this cometh" they shall know that Jehovah God is supreme, and back of all the judgments of the trouble time.

PASTOR RUSSELL DEAD, BUT SPEAKING AGAIN

24:25, 26. **Also, thou son of man, shall it not be in the day when I take from them their strength, the joy of their glory, the desire of their eyes, and that whereupon they set their minds, their sons and their daughters. That he that escapeth in that day shall come unto thee, to cause thee to hear it with thine ears?**—Also, in the year 1918, when God destroys the churches wholesale and the church members by millions, it shall be that any that escape shall come to the works of Pastor Russell to learn the meaning of the downfall of "Christianity."

24:27. **In that day shall thy mouth be opened to him which is escaped, and thou shalt speak, and be no more dumb: and thou shalt be a sign unto them; and they shall know that I am the Lord.**—Pastor Russell's voice has been stilled in death; and his voice is, comparatively speaking, dumb to what it will be. In the time of revolution and anarchy he shall speak, and be no more dumb to those that escape the destruction of that day. Pastor Russell shall "be a sign unto them," shall tell them the truth about the Divine appointment of the trouble, as they consult his books, scattered to the number of ten million throughout Christendom. His words shall be a sign of hope unto them, enabling them to see the bright side of the cloud and to look forward with anticipation to the glorious Kingdom of God to be established. Then "they shall know the Lord."

" Build thee more stately mansions, O my soul,
  As the swift seasons roll!
  Leave thy low vaulted past!
Let each new temple, nobler than the last,
Shut thee from heaven with a dome more vast,
  Till thou at length art free,
Leaving thine outgrown shell by life's unresting sea."

1917 edition

Who was to be resurrected?
When was this resurrection to take place?
What does 1925 signify?

Millions Now Living Will Never Die

seventy jubilees kept. (Jeremiah 25:11; 2 Chronicles 36:17-21) A simple calculation of these jubilees brings us to this important fact: Seventy jubilees of fifty years each would be a total of 3500 years. That period of time beginning 1575 before A. D. 1 of necessity would end in the fall of the year 1925, at which time the type ends and the great antitype must begin. What, then, should we expect to take place? In the type there must be a full restoration; therefore the great antitype must mark the beginning of restoration of all things. The chief thing to be restored is the human race to life; and since other Scriptures definitely fix the fact that there will be a resurrection of Abraham, Isaac, Jacob and other faithful ones of old, and that these will have the first favor, we may expect 1925 to witness the return of these faithful men of Israel from the condition of death, being resurrected and fully restored to perfect humanity and made the visible, legal representatives of the new order of things on earth.

Messiah's kingdom once established, Jesus and his glorified church constituting the great Messiah, shall minister the blessings to the people they have so long desired and hoped for and prayed might come. And when that time comes, there will be peace and not war, as the prophet beautifully states: "In the last days it shall come to pass, that the mountain of the house of the Lord shall be established in the top of the mountains, and it shall be exalted above

62

the hills; and people shall flow unto it. And
many nations shall come, and say, Come, and
let us go up to the mountain of the Lord, and to
the house of the God of Jacob; and he will teach
us of his ways, and we will walk in his paths:
for the law shall go forth of Zion, and the word
of the Lord from Jerusalem. And he shall judge
among many people, and rebuke strong nations
afar off; and they shall beat their swords into
plowshares, and their spears into pruninghooks;
nation shall not lift up a sword against nation,
neither shall they learn war any more. But they
shall sit every man under his vine and under his
fig tree; and none shall make them afraid; for
the mouth of the Lord of hosts hath spoken it."
—Micah 4:1-4.

EARTHLY RULERS

As we have heretofore stated, the great jubilee cycle is due to begin in 1925. At that time
the earthly phase of the kingdom shall be recognized. The Apostle Paul in the eleventh chapter
of Hebrews names a long list of faithful men
who died before the crucifixion of the Lord and
before the beginning of the selection of the
church. These can never be a part of the heavenly class; they had no heavenly hopes; but God
has in store something good for them. They are
to be resurrected as perfect men and constitute
the princes or rulers in the earth, according to
his promise. (Psalm 45:16; Isaiah 32:1; Matthew 8:11) Therefore we may confidently expect that 1925 will mark the return of Abraham,

Isaac, Jacob and the faithful prophets of old, particularly those named by the Apostle in Hebrews chapter eleven, to the condition of human perfection.

RECONSTRUCTION

All the statesmen of the world, all the political economists, all the thoughtful men and women, recognize the fact that the conditions existing prior to the war have passed away and that a new order of things must be put in vogue. All such recognize that this is a period now marking the beginning of reconstruction. The great difficulty is that these men are exercising only human wisdom and have ignored the divine arrangement. We are indeed at the time of reconstruction, the reconstruction not only of a few things, but of all things. The reconstruction will not consist of patching up old and broken down systems and forms and arrangements, but the establishment of a new and righteous one under the great ruler Christ Jesus, the Prince of Peace. The Apostle Peter at Pentecost, speaking under divine inspiration, and referring to that time, said: "Times of refreshing shall come from the presence of the Lord; and he shall send Jesus Christ, which before was preached unto you: whom the heaven must receive [retain] until the times of restitution of all things, which God hath spoken by the mouth of all his holy prophets since the world began". —Acts 3:19-21.

THE WATCH TOWER

desperation they will seek vengeance against the French. It is a deplorable state of affairs.

EUROPE A BOILING CAULDRON

Austria is panic-stricken, and another revolution is expected any day. In Italy the revolutionists threaten to overturn the government, and fear has taken hold upon every one who is in power. In fact all Europe is a boiling pot, with the [...] increasing. If any one w[...] through Europe and [...] has ended, that the day [...] the Messianic kingdom is at the door, then he has read the Bible in vain. The physical facts show beyond question of a doubt that 1914 ended the Gentile times; and as the Lord foretold, the old order is being destroyed by war, famine, pestilence, and revolution.

> What did 1914 end?
> What date is distinctly indicated in Scripture?
> When will the "crisis" be past?

The date 1925 is even more distinctly indicated by the Scriptures because it is fixed by the law God gave to Israel. Viewing the present situation in Europe, one wonders how it will be possible to hold back the explosion much longer; and that even before 1925 the great crisis will be reached and probably passed. The present conditions are strengthening to the faith of the Christian [...] with others of the groaning [...] : Prince of Peace bring order to the people.
[...] w accorded the followers of [...] opportunity of holding aloof from the strife and turmoil of earth and bringing to the people the message of peace and salvation and saying unto those of nominal Zion who have been looking to th Lord: 'Behold, the Lord is here; behold thy God reigneth!'

(To be continued.)

A REFRESHING SEASON

"And Jesus said unto them, Come ye yourselves apart into a desert place, and rest a while; for there were many coming and going, and they had no leisure so much as to eat."—Mark 6:31.

and to his plans and purposes for the deliverance of humanity into the realm of life and happiness. Thus using the mind, we ascertain what is the good and acceptable and perfect will of God concerning us and our course as Christians; and as we follow his will, the transformation progresses from ...., by the spirit of ...

likeness of our Lord will desire to hold together and will hold together. Appreciating the proper relationship existing between the members of the body leads each one thus appreciat... be loyal to every other member..., the spirit of love, each ...; and all are held together, ... the Head

> What date is "definitely settled" in Scripture?
> What will be the response of the nations to this date?

QUESTION AND ANSWER

Question: Did the order go forth eight months ago to the Pilgrims to cease talking about 1925? Have we more reason, or as much, to believe the kingdom will be established in 1925 than Noah had to believe that there would be a flood?

Answer: It is surprising how reports get abroad. There was never at any time any intimation to the Pilgrim brethren that they should cease talking about 1925. Anyone who has made the statement that such an instruction was sent out has made it without any authority or excuse or cause.

Our thought is, that 1925 is definitely settled by the Scriptures, marking the end of the typical jubilees

Just exactly what will happen at that time no one can tell to a certainty; but we expect such a climax in the affairs of the world that the people will begin to realize the presence of the Lord and his kingdom power. He is already present, as we know, and has taken unto himself his power and begun his reign. He has come to his temple. He is dashing to pieces the nations. Every Christian ought to be content, then, to do with his might what his hands find to do, without stopping to quibble about what is going to happen on a certain date.

As to Noah, the Christian now has much more upon which to base his faith than Noah had (so far as the Scriptures reveal) upon which to base his faith in a coming deluge.

The WATCH TOWER

AND HERALD OF CHRIST'S PRESENCE

Vol. XLVI

January 1, 1925

No. 1

"The Spirit of the Lord God is upon me; because the Lord hath anointed me to preach the good tidings unto the meek:... to proclaim... the day of vengeance of our God; to comfort all that mourn."—Isaiah 61:1, 2.

WORK FOR THE ANOINTED

THE paramount duty devolving upon every intelligent creature is to glorify God. It is the expressed will of Jehovah that th............ outworking of his .... divine pr......... ture then of God. hovah's fa to the glo divine plan devotion to the Lord and to his cause, will accomplish for the faithful this desired end.

What was to happen in 1925 according to the Watchtower?

When 1925 arrived, what did the Watchtower say?

"The year 1925 is here. With great expectation Christians have looked forward to this year. Many have confidently expected that all members of the body of Christ will be changed to heavenly glory during the year. This may be accomplished. It may not be. In his own due time God will accomplish his purposes concerning his own people. Christians should not be so deeply concerned about what may transpire during this year that they would fail to joyfully do what the lord would have them to do.

"A Christian is one who is begotten and anointed of the holy spirit. He has agreed to do the will of

authority. A ....y with the ....s prompted so to do by unselfish ...... on one or more crea
..... the doing of certain mission will, if he is
It the terms or pro ascertain whether or
..... duties.

ne anointed ones must hold fast to that which they have learned, to wit: That the Lord Jesus Christ, the Redeemer and Head of the Church, is now present and has taken his power and begun his reign; that the great fundamental truths of God's plan have been restored to the Church, which restoration was foreshadowed by the work of Elijah; that the Lord has come to his temple and is examining the members thereof; that the present work of the Church this side of the vail was foreshadowed by the work of Elisha, who did both a slaying and a comforting work; that the part of the commission given to the Church yet unfulfilled is: To declare the day of vengeance of our God, and to comfort all that mourn.

"An abundant entrance into the kingdom of our Lord and Savior is the sincere desire of each one of the anointed. To this end it is essential that he hold fast is described in the S——

From what date can we say the second coming or presence of Christ took place?
When was Satan ousted from heaven?
When did the Lord come to His temple?

————— is given to the gathering together of his true followers and separating them from the nominal followers, and making ready conditions to take charge of the world's affairs. The Scriptural proof is that the period of his presence and the day of God's preparation is a period from 1874 A. D. forward. The second coming of the Lord, therefore, began in 1874; and that date and the years 1914 to 1918 are specially marked dates with reference to his coming.

The "world" includes both visible and invisible governments; hence it means heaven and earth. For centuries Satan has been the invisible ruler of governmental organizations on earth; and, being invisible to man, he has also ruled man's heaven. The time must come when Satan's world must end, and when he is ousted from heaven; and the Scriptural proof is that the beginning of such ousting took place in 1914.

The temple of the Lord means his approved followers, those constituting "the body of Christ". The time must arrive when Christ Jesus comes to his temple to take an account with his followers. The Scriptural proof supports the conclusion that the coming to his temple was in the year 1918. Later there must follow the complete overthrow of Satan's organization, both visible and invisible, and the establishment of an invisible and visible government of righteousness.

Jehovah caused his prophets to write concerning the coming of Christ, and their writings were couched in "dark sayings" or prophetic phrase. Prophecy can cleaners, wireless telegraphy and ——

The most

When was Christ's coming due?

...g of the Lord. It is de-
...ed by the prophet as a blessed time. Daniel then
says: "Blessed is he that waiteth, and cometh to the
thousand three hundred and five and thirty [1335]
days." (Dan. 12:12) The watchers here are, without
question, those who were instructed by the Lord to
watch for his return. This date, therefore, when understood, would certainly fix the time when the Lord
is due at his second appearing. Applying the same
rule then, of a day for a year, 1335 days after 539
A. D. brings us to 1874 A. D., at which time, according
to Biblical chronology, the Lord's second presence
was due. If this calculation is correct, from that time
forward we ought to be able to find evidence marking
the Lord's second presence.

There are two important dates here that we must
not confuse, but clearly differentiate; namely, the beginning of "the time of the end" and the beginning
of the presence of the Lord. "The time of the end"
embraces a period from 1799 A. D. to the time of the
complete overthrow of Satan's empire and the establishment of the kingdom of Messiah. The time of the
Lord's second presence dates from 1874 and is during
the latter part of the period known as "the time of
the end".

Preparation

· The Scriptures designate a specific period of time as
"the day of his preparation". Within that period of
time God draws his people together and gives them a
knowledge of his plan and purposes, then in due time
Christ Jesus suddenly comes to his temple, gathers together those who are in the covenant by sacrifice, and
brings them into the temple condition. It is a time

nated in the Scriptures under the symbol of "beasts".
The Prophet Daniel (7:7, 8) describes a "fourth
beast, dreadful and terrible". This terrible beast was
a form of government composed of the ...

compon...

What date marked "the beginning of the time
of the end"?

... united. Of this

... ...ity we see the Papacy, the ecclesiastical
element, in the saddle, riding and directing everything. The date of its beginning was at the overthrow
of the Ostrogothic monarchy, which occurred in 539
A. D.

The Prophet Daniel was given a vision of the events
following. Yet he did not understand them; and he
says: "I Daniel looked, and, behold, there stood other
two, the one on this side of the bank of the river, and
the other on that side of the bank of the river. And
one said to the man clothed in linen, which was upon
the waters of the river, How long shall it be to the
end of these wonders? And I heard the man clothed
in linen, which was upon the waters of the river, when
he held up his right hand and his left hand unto
heaven, and sware by him that liveth for ever, that
it shall be for a time, times and an half."—Dan.
12:5-7.

In Biblical symbology a "time" means a year of
twelve months of thirty days each, or 360 days. Each
day is considered for a year, as the prophet says: "I
have appointed thee each day for a year." (Ezek. 4:
6) Here are mentioned, then, three and a half times
of 360 prophetic days each, or a total of 1260 prophetic days, which would mark the beginning of the
time of the end of this beastly order. Twelve hundred
and sixty years from 539 A. D. brings us to 1799,
which is another proof that 1799 definitely marks the
beginning of "the time of the end". This also shows

70

that it is from the date 539 A. D. that the other prophetic days of Daniel must be counted.

The understanding of the prophecies with reference to "the time of the end" and the Lord's presence was purposely concealed by Jehovah until the due time. Daniel desired to know what would be the end of these things, but God said to him: "But thou, O Daniel, shut up the words, and seal the book, even to the time of the end." (Dan. 12: 4) It is reasonable to expect that Jehovah would indicate something by which "the time of the end" could be discerned when it arrived. He did not say to Daniel to look for some words emblazoned across the sky telling that the end had come, but told him to look for such evidences as could be seen and understood by men who were familiar with the prophecies, and who in the light of the prophecies should be watching for their fulfilment. God did not expect Daniel to see and understand these prophecies in his day, for he said: "Go thy way, Daniel; for the words are closed up and sealed till the time of the end."—Dan. 12: 9.

When that time should arrive, what was to be expected? Jehovah answers: "Many shall run to and fro, and knowledge shall be increased." (Dan. 12: 4) From shortly after 1799, the date of the beginning of "the time of the end", we should expect to find an increase of knowledge, particularly with reference to the Bible. Prior to that time the people had been kept in ignorance of the Bible. It was the practice of the Papacy to forbid any one aside from the clergy class to have access to the Bible; in fact, to have in possession a copy of the Bible was made a crime under the Roman law, subjecting the offender to heavy penalties.

In 1799 the beastly power of Rome, predominated by the Papal system, received a deadly wound. The people had been taught to believe in the divine right the same class were, however, to wit: faithful Christians who, believing and obeying God's commands, were hated by all the nations involved in the war and were persecuted and imprisoned, and many of them killed.

The Master showed that about this same time professed Christians would betray and hate one another, and that many would be turned away from following after the Lord because of false teachers and because of hatred, but that some would faithfully endure until the end. These conditions have obtained, particularly since 1917 and thereafter. This is but corroborative proof of the Lord's presence at the end of the world.

Jehovah having promised Abraham and his "seed" the land of Palestine when the Gentile times should end and when he "whose right it is" should come, we should now expect some manifestation of God's favor toward Israel in returning that people to the possession of the land of Palestine. Jesus referred to this same matter in connection with his presence at the end of the world, when he said: "Jerusalem shall be trodden down of the Gentiles, until the times of the Gentiles be fulfilled." (Luke 21: 24) The Lord's presence began in 1874, as heretofore stated. It was in 1878 that there was the first manifestation of God's favor returning to Israel. This was marked by reason of the efforts made on behalf of the Jews by Disraeli, then the prime minister of the British Empire. A few years thereafter a movement designated "Zionism" began to restore the people of Israel to their land.

During the World War, to wit, November 2, 1917, which was the beginning of the Jewish year 1918, the British Empire expressed its willingness for the Jews to establish in Palestine a government of their own. Other leading nations have acquiesced. In the spring of the year 1918, the Jews began to rebuild Palestine; and now it is a commonly known fact that thousands of Jews have returned to Palestine and they are buying the land and building houses and otherwise improving the country exactly as the Lord foretold. This is another physical fact or circumstantial proof of the Lord's presence at the end of the world.

Another evidence mentioned by Jesus was the fact that following the war, and during his presence at the end of the world, there should be "upon the earth distress of nations, with perplexity; . . . men's hearts failing them for fear, and for looking after those things which are coming on the earth". (Luke 21: 25, 26) He had stated that the World War was the "beginning of sorrows", and now he shows that the distress must continue. It needs no proof that all the nations are today in perplexity, and that men are distrustful one of another and fearful of what they see approaching. This is another strong corroborative proof of the Lord's presence and of the end of the world, beginning in 1914.

Coming to His Temple

The new creation is likened unto a building or temple, and is called "the temple of God". (2 Cor. 6: 16; Eph. 2: 18-22; 1 Pet. 2: 5) It is the house of God, of which Christ Jesus is the Head. (Heb. 3: 6; 1 Cor. 3: 16, 17) It is this temple class to whom the Lord committed his goods, to wit, the interests of his kingdom during the Christian era. Jesus taught often by parables; and by at least two parables he described himself as a man taking a long journey, and then after a long period of time returning to take account with his servants. (Matt. 25: 14-30; Luke 19: 12-26) These are known as the parables of the talents and the pounds. The events transpiring in fulfilment of these prophetic parables show the Lord's coming to his temple.

308   *Creation*

The events transpiring during the three and one-half years of the ministry of Christ Jesus, from 29 to 33 A. D., find a parallel in events at the close of the Christian era and during his second presence. Jesus was anointed as King at the Jordan. Three and one-half years thereafter he appeared in the literal temple of Jerusalem and cleared out the impostors and approved the faithful. (Matt. 21:1-13) As hereinbefore stated, Christ took his power to reign in 1914; at which time, he had said, the nations would be angry. (Rev. 11:17,18) Three and one-half years thereafter, to wit, in 1918, he was due to come and did come to his temple. Circumstantial evidence, which constitutes the physical facts, proves the correctness of this conclusion.

Jehovah sent his beloved Son as his great Deputy or Ambassador, called his "Messenger", to do his preparatory work. That work must be done, and it *was* done, from 1874 to 1914 in particular; and then followed a period of expectancy in which the members of the body of Christ on earth were anxiously waiting for him to set up his kingdom; and while they were so waiting, he suddenly came to his temple. This order of procedure was foretold by God through his prophet. "Behold, I will send my messenger, and he shall prepare the way before me: and the Lord, whom ye seek, shall suddenly come to his temple, even the messenger of the covenant, whom ye delight in: behold, he shall come, saith the Lord of hosts."—Mal. 3:1.

Exactly as the prophet foretold, the events did transpire. From 1914 to 1918 the true followers of Jesus on earth were saying that the time for the King's reign is here, and were eagerly waiting for the fulfilment of their hearts' desires. And then in 1918, suddenly fell upon them a time of great testing. God through his prophet had foretold that the coming of the Lord to his temple would be a time of trial and testing upon the members of the new creation. "But who may abide the day of his coming? and who shall stand when he appeareth? for he is like a refiner's fire, and like fullers' sope: and he shall sit as a refiner and purifier of silver; and he shall purify the sons of Levi, and purge them as gold and silver, that they may offer unto the Lord an offering in righteousness." —Mal. 3:2, 3.

It is manifest that the word "silver" in this text is used as a symbol of truth. (Ps. 12:6) This prophecy would indicate that the true followers of Christ would have a clearer vision of the truth after the Lord's coming to his temple in 1918. This is also corroborated by Rev. 11:19. The facts show that following that time they did have a clearer understanding of God's plan. The "sons of Levi" mentioned in the above prophecy foreshadowed and represent the new creation, and the 'purifying' of these shows that the coming of the Lord to his temple would be a time of trial for his true followers. This parallels and was foreshadowed by the purifying of the literal temple in Jerusalem in 33 A. D. The purpose of purifying the temple class is that the Lord might have a faithful and true class of witnesses to testify to his name and his work, before the final demonstration of his power in the great time of trouble.

Another prophet of God corroborates the above and shows the purpose of the Lord's coming to his temple. "The Lord is in his holy temple, the Lord's throne is in heaven: his eyes behold, his eyelids try, the children of men." (Ps. 11:4) If the known physical facts fit the prophecy, such must be a fulfilment thereof; and if such have occurred since 1918, that would be further proof that the Lord came to his temple at that time.

parable as the "wheat" and the "tares" growing in
the same field. He declared they must continue th---
to grow together until the end ...
13·24·30··

As late as 1929, what date signified the second
coming or presence of the Lord?

...... inter-
......uence and personal flattery.
Under the influence and control of the enemy Satan,
they caused the truth to become obscure and to be
seen very dimly.

Again attention is called to the words of Jesus, the
great Prophet, who with authority from Jehovah said
to his disciples: "I go to prepare a place for you.
And if I go . . . I will come again and receive you
unto myself." It should therefore be expected that
the coming again of the Lord would mark the beginning of a better understanding of God's Word. In
harmony with this, Peter at Pentecost uttered a
prophecy saying: "Times of refreshing shall come
from the presence [face] of the Lord [Jehovah]; and
he shall send Jesus Christ, which before was preached
unto you; whom the heaven must receive [retain]
until the times of restitution of all things, which God
hath spoken by the mouth of all his holy prophets
since the world began." (Acts 3:19-21) In this the
apostle clearly foretells a time of refreshing to the
people of the Lord, and that the time would be at the
second coming of the Lord Jesus.

That would not mean that Jesus must be bodily
present again on the earth, because with him distance
is no barrier. He is a spirit being of the divine nature,
and his power is without limitation, regardless of his
actual bodily position. Being clothed with all power
in heaven and in earth, he could administer the affairs
of the church from one point as well as from another.

The apostle's words mean that, at a stated time and acting in accord with Jehovah's orders, Christ Jesus would begin to minister to those consecrated to God and give them refreshing. What would be the nature of that refreshing?

Peter mentions "restitution", which would mean a restoring of that which had been taken away or hidden, and would necessarily include the truth that was hidden during the "dark ages". On another occasion Jesus said that 'Elijah must first come and restore all things'. (Matt. 17:11) Elijah was a prophet of God who did a restitution work in his time, in that he restored to the Israelites an understanding of the truth concerning God and their covenant relationship with God. (1 Ki. 18:39) His work was prophetic and foretold that the Lord would restore his truth to his own people. After Elijah was dead, Malachi prophesied that God would send Elijah the prophet before the great and dreadful day of the Lord. (Mal. 4:5, 6) That prophecy is proof that another should do a work similar to that done by Elijah, but on a far greater scale and of much more importance.

The restitution or restoring of all things, of which Jesus spoke, and also that mentioned by the Apostle Peter, must begin with the restoring to the people of God the truths that had been hidden during the dark ages. That restitution work would progress during the manifestation of the second presence of Jesus Christ. It would be expected that the days of understanding of the prophecies would begin sometime after the manifestation of the Lord's second presence, and the understanding would continue to increase thereafter.

The Scriptural proof is that the second presence of the Lord Jesus Christ began in 1874 A.D. This proof

Why did the Watchtower build Beth Sarim?

BETH-SARIM

BETH-SARIM

At San Diego, California, there is a small piece of land, on which, in the year 1929, there was built a house, which is called and known as Beth-Sarim. The Hebrew words *Beth Sarim* mean "House of the Princes"; and the purpose of acquiring that property and building the house was that there might be some tangible proof that there are those on earth today who fully believe God and Christ Jesus and in His kingdom, and who believe that the faithful men of old will soon be resurrected by the Lord, be back on earth, and take charge of the visible affairs of earth. The title to Beth-Sarim is vested in the WATCH TOWER BIBLE & TRACT SOCIETY in trust, to be used by the president of the Society and his assistants for the present, and thereafter to be for ever at the disposal of the aforementioned princes on the earth. To be sure, everything then on the earth will belong to the Lord, and neither the Lord nor the princes need others to build houses for them; but it was thought well and pleasing to God that the aforementioned house be built as a testimony to the name of Jehovah and showing faith in his announced purposes. The house has served as a testimony to many persons throughout the earth, and while the unbelievers have mocked concerning it and spoken contemptuously of it, yet it stands there as a testimony to Jehovah's name; and if and when the princes do return and some of them occupy the property, such will be a confirmation of the faith and hope that induced the building of Beth-Sarim.

sage. (Ps. 91:1-9; Isa. 51:16) The fact that Ezekiel survived the destruction of Jerusalem indicates that some of the remnant at least will be on the earth after the destruction of Christendom.

"Also, thou son of man, shall it not be in the day when I take from them their strength, the joy of their glory, the desire of their

In 1931, what dates were said to be definitely fixed in the Scriptures?

... . (24:25, 26;

..., Ezekiel, by commandment, spoke the word of prophecy, and Jehovah would have that word verified by eye witnesses who survived the disaster upon Jerusalem and who would testify that Ezekiel had spoken truthfully. Thus is indicated what shall come to pass after the fall of Christendom, and thus God "confirmeth the word of his servant, and performeth the counsel of his messengers". (Isa. 44:26) In such manner God will prove to the survivors that there has been a class of people in the land who have been and are faithful to him and who have truthfully proclaimed his word.—Ezek. 33:33.

These scriptures support the conclusion that the "servant", that is, Jehovah's faithful witnesses, whom Ezekiel foreshadowed, will be on earth for some time after the destruction of Christendom, and that the survivors will be eye-witnesses of that destruction and will seek out the remnant and will confess that God has used the remnant to declare his truth.

There was a measure of disappointment on the part of Jehovah's faithful ones on earth concerning the years 1914, 1918 and 1925, which disappointment lasted for a time. Later the faithful learned that these

(published in 1931)

dates were definitely fixed in the Scriptures; and they also learned to quit fixing dates for the future and predicting what would come to pass on a certain date, but to rely (and they do rely) upon the Word of God as to the events that must come to pass. Jehovah has spoken his word and will perform it, and the Scriptures seem clearly to indicate that Jehovah will grant to his faithful witnesses the privilege of seeing his great "act", thereby proving that his witnesses have spoken his word of truth according to his will; and that this he will do before his witnesses are "changed" into the glorious organism like unto Christ Jesus'. This is not predicting dates, but is merely calling attention to events that must come to pass because clearly set forth in God's Word.

Now the witnesses of Jehovah are not in good repute with men. There are many who believe the truth but who shun the witnesses of Jehovah because of fear of losing their reputation or their property. By so doing they are moved by selfishness, of course; but as surely as the witnesses of Jehovah speak his truth, just so surely God will make the people come to know that such witnesses have spoken truthfully. This will not be that the witnesses may have an exaltation amongst men, but that the people may know that God has had witnesses amongst them.

Great is the privilege to now be a witness for Jehovah. Only those who have full faith and confidence in and love for God and his kingdom will now declare the truth with boldness. This is the day of judgment, and those who really love God will speak with boldness. (1 John 4: 17, 18) Others who have received the truth but not the love of it will go to the rulers in twentieth century an independent study has been carried on that does not blindly follow some traditional chronological calculations of Christendom, and the published timetable resulting from this independent study gives the date of man's creation as 4026 B.C.E.† According to this trustworthy Bible chronology six thousand years from man's creation will end in 1975, and the seventh period of a thousand years of human history will begin in the fall of 1975 C.E.

⁴² So six thousand years of man's existence on earth will soon be up, yes, within this generation. Jehovah God is timeless, as it is ----'--

90·1 ·· ··

What date fixed the end of six thousand years of man's existence on the earth? What date would be appropriate for the millennium to begin?

--- ------ue

--- -- ·· from the standpoint of Jehovah God these passing six thousand years of man's existence are but as six days of twenty-four hours, for this same psalm (verses 3, 4) goes on to say: "You make mortal man go back to crushed matter, and you say: 'Go back, you sons of men.' For a thousand years are in your eyes but as yesterday when it is past, and as a watch during the night." So in not many years within our own generation we are reaching what Jehovah God could view as the seventh day of man's existence.

Swensko, published in Lund, Sweden, in 1862 (pages CXXI-CXXVIII). This differs from Ussher's Chronology by four years.

† See "Chart of Outstanding Historical Dates" on page 292, in the chapter entitled "Measuring Events in the Stream of Time," of the book *All Scripture Is Inspired of God and Beneficial*," published in 1963 by the Watch Tower Bible & Tract Society of Pennsylvania.

42. From the standpoint of Jehovah God, how long has man's existence been?

82

[43] How appropriate it would be for Jehovah God to make of this coming seventh period of a thousand years a sabbath period of rest and release, a great Jubilee sabbath for the proclaiming of liberty throughout the earth to all its inhabitants! This would be most timely for mankind. It would also be most fitting on God's part, for, remember, mankind has yet ahead of it what the last book of the Holy Bible speaks of as the reign of Jesus Christ over earth for a thousand years, the millennial reign of Christ. Prophetically Jesus Christ, when on earth nineteen centuries ago, said concerning himself: "For Lord of the sabbath is what the Son of man is." (Matthew 12:8) It would not be by mere chance or accident but would be according to the loving purpose of Jehovah God for the reign of Jesus Christ, the "Lord of the sabbath," to run parallel with the seventh millennium of man's existence.

[44] The Jubilee year of God's ancient law was a "shadow of the good things to come." The substantial reality that it foreshadowed must yet without fail be introduced for the good of all the groaning human creation. The blessed time for its introduction is fast approaching. Shortly, within our own generation, the symbolical trumpet will be sounded by divine power, proclaiming "liberty in the land to all its inhabitants." (Leviticus 25:8-10) God foresaw the need for this and had it foreshadowed in his ancient law given through the prophet Moses. As his law foreshadowed this coming great worldwide Jubilee, he has laid the full legal basis for its full, glorious realization. Consequently there is now every reason why the human creation will yet be set free, not by men, but by Almighty God. The long-awaited time for this is at hand!

43. What act on God's part would be most timely for mankind and most fitting in the fulfillment of Jehovah's purpose?
44. Why can we have strong confidence that the human creation will yet be set free, not by men, but by God?

HOW ARE YOU USING YOUR LIFE?

IS IT not apparent that most of mankind are living their lives for themselves? They are using their lives as *they* see fit, without concern for others. But what about us? The apostle Paul wrote to fellow servants of Jehovah, saying: "None of us, in fact, lives with regard to himself only, and no one dies with regard to himself only; for both if we live, we live to Jehovah, and if we die, we die to Jehovah. Therefore both if we live and if we die, we belong to Jehovah."—Rom. 14:7, 8.

This is something for all of us to give serious thought to: It would be entirely inappropriate for us, while professing to be Jehovah's people, to try to live our lives with regard to ourselves only. As the apostle Paul wrote: "You do not belong to yourselves, for you were bought with a ~~~~ all means, glorify God."

Are ~~~
has ~~~
Hir ~~~
own ~~~
have ~~~
oppo ~~~
3:16, ~~~
ing p ~~~
to wa~~~ ~~~ not cause you to wa~~~ ~~~ehovah your deep appreciation? The apostle Peter noted that if we have the proper mental disposition we will be moved to "live the remainder of [our] time in the flesh, no more for the desires of men, *but for God's will.*"—1 Pet. 4:2.

Is that what you are doing? Are you living no longer simply to satisfy personal ambitions or desires, but to do God's will? Are there ways in which you could share more fully in doing the will of God?

God's Will for Us

Jehovah makes clear in his Word that his will for us today includes accomplishing a great work of Kingdom-preaching before the end of this system comes. (Matt. 24:14) Jesus Christ did a similar work. He said: "Also to other cities I must declare the good news of the kingdom of God, *because for this I was sent forth.*"—Luke 4:43.

Jesus did not hold back, but was whole-souled in his service to God. When we read the historical accounts of his ministry in the Gospels, how impressed we are with his energy and zeal in doing the Kingdom-preaching! Jesus knew that he had only a short time, and he did not spare himself in finishing his assignment. Should we not today be imitating his example, especially since we have such a short time left now in which to complete the Kingdom-preaching?

Yes, the end of this system is so very near! Is that not reason to increase our activity? In this regard we can learn something from a runner who puts on a final burst of speed near the finish of a race ~~~ ~~~us, who apparently st~~~ during ~~~ 27 per~~~ is de~~~ ~~~arthly ~~~ 1-15: ~~~ 30. ~~~ ing ~~~ may find ~~~ more time and energy ~~~ing during this final period before the present system ends. Many of our brothers and sisters are doing just that. This is evident from the rapidly increasing number of pioneers.

Yes, since the summer of 1973 there have been new peaks in pioneers every month. Now there are 20,394 regular and special pioneers in the United States, an all-time peak. That is 5,190 more than there were in February 1973! A 34-percent increase! Does that not warm our hearts? Reports are heard of brothers selling their homes and property and planning to finish out the rest of their days in this old system in the pioneer service. Certainly this is a fine way to spend the short time remaining before the wicked world's end.—1 John 2:17.

Circumstances such as poor health or responsibilities in connection with your family may limit what you can do in the field ministry. And yet, the pioneer ranks include many who have health limitations, as well as some persons with families. But these brothed to be October 5 (Julian) or September 29 (Gregorian) 537 B.C.E.—Ezra 1:1-4; 3:1-6.

²⁴ Here, then ⸺⸺⸺⸺ is ar⸺⸺ sever⸺⸺ Juda⸺⸺ 537.⸺⸺ simple⸺⸺ sevent⸺⸺ years ⸺gan. One has only to add

Why did Jehovah's Witnesses look forward to 1975? When were the 6,000 years since Adam's creation to be up?

70 to 537 to get 607. So about October 607 B.C.E. ᵗʰᵃ⸺ he land ⸺⸺ing out ⸺⸺plished ⸺⸺ 607 B.C.E ⸺⸺ becom ⸺⸺ ⸺⸺ the following article, we seek an answer to the provocative question, When was Adam created?

24. So when did the seventy years of desolation begin, and when did they end?

25. The answer to what question is related to year 607 B.C.E.?

WHY ARE YOU LOOKING FORWARD TO

1975?

WHAT about all this talk concerning the year 1975? Lively discussions, some based on speculation, have burst into flame during recent months among serious students of the Bible. Their interest has been kindled by the belief that 1975 will mark the end of 6,000 years of human history since Adam's creation. The nearness of such an important date indeed fires the imagination and presents unlimited possibilities for discussion.

² But wait! How do we know their calculations are correct? What basis is there for saying Adam was created nearly 5,993 years ago? Does the one Book that can be implicitly trusted for its truthful historical accuracy, namely, the Inspired Word of Jehovah, the Holy Bible, give support and credence to such a conclusion?

³ In the marginal references of the Protestant *Authorized* or *King James Version,* and in the footnotes of certain editions of the Catholic *Douay* version, the date of man's creation is said to be 4004 B.C.E. This marginal date, however, is no part of the inspired text of the Holy Scriptures, since it was first suggested more than fifteen centuries after the last Bible writer died, and was not added to any edition of the Bible until 1701 C.E. It is an insertion based upon the conclusions of an Irish prelate, the Anglican Archbishop James Ussher (1581-1656). Ussher's chronology was only one of the many sincere efforts made during the past centuries to determine the time of Adam's creation. A hundred years ago when a count was taken, no less than 140 different timetables had been published by se-

1, 2. (a) What has sparked special interest in the year 1975, and with what results? (b) But what questions are raised?

3. Is the date for Adam's creation as found in many copies of the Bible part of the Inspired Scriptures, and do all agree on the date?

was long before the Israelites entered Egypt.—Gen. 21:8, 9.

²¹ Well, then, how long were the Israelites down in Egypt as alien residents? Exodus 12:40, 41 says: "And the dwelling of the sons of Israel, who had dwelt in Egypt, was four hundred and th⸍ And it came ⸍⸍ fo⸍ ca⸍ ar⸍ of ⸍

²² ⸍⸍⸍gint reads: "Bu⸍ ⸍⸍⸍g of the sons of Israel which they [and their fathers, Alexandrine MS] dwelt in the land of Egypt AND IN THE LAND OF CANAAN [was] four hundred and thirty years long." The Samaritan Pentateuch reads: "IN THE LAND OF CANAAN and in the land of Egypt." Thus both of these versions, which are based on Hebrew texts older than the Masoretic, include the words "in the land of Canaan" together with the word "Egypt."

²³ From the time that Abraham entered Canaan until Isaac's birth was 25 years;* from that time until Jacob's birth, 60 more years; and after that it was another 130 years before Jacob entered Egypt. All together this makes a total of 215 years, exactly half of the 430 years, spent in Canaan before moving into Egypt. (Gen. 12:4; 21:5; 25:26; 47:9) The apostle Paul, under inspiration, also confirms that from the making of the Abrahamic covenant at the time the patriarch moved into Canaan, it was 430 years down to the institution of the Law covenant.—Gal. 3:17.

---

* Incidentally, adding 5 more years to the 25, and bringing it down to the time Isaac was weaned, makes a total of 30 years. This accounts for the difference between the 400 years (Gen. 15:13; Acts 7:6) and the 430 years (Ex. 12:30; Gal. 3:17).

21, 22. Were the Israelites 430 years in Egypt exclusively, and how do certain ancient manuscripts shed light on this point?
23. (a) So how long were the Israelites actually in Egypt, and how does Paul confirm this? (b) Explain the difference between the 400 and the 430 years mentioned in the Scriptures.

²⁴ By adding this 430 years to the 1513 it puts us back to 1943 B.C.E., the time when Abraham first entered Canaan following the death of his f⸍⸍ r Terah in Haran, Meso⸍⸍ only a mat- ⸍⸍ a few gen- ectly. The ⸍apters 11 ⸍d as fol-

What was possibly to happen by the autumn of 1975? Could anyone see beyond 1975? What was 1975 to signify?

⸍⸍ ₒₒd

To Arpachshad's birth (Gen. 11:10)	2 years
To birth of Shelah (11:12)	35 "
To birth of Eber (11:14)	30 "
To birth of Peleg (11:26)	34 "
To birth of Reu (11:18)	30 "
To birth of Serug (11:20)	32 "
To birth of Nahor (11:22)	30 "
To birth of Terah (11:24)	29 "
To death of Terah in Haran, and Abram's departure to Canaan at age of 75 (11:32; 12:4)	205 "
Total	427 years

²⁵ Adding these 427 years to the year 1943 B.C.E. dates the beginning of the Deluge at 2370 B.C.E., 4,337 years ago.

6,000 YEARS FROM ADAM'S CREATION

²⁶ In a similar manner it is only necessary to add up the following years involving ten pre-Flood generations to get the date of Adam's creation, namely:

From Adam's creation

To birth of Seth (Gen. 5:3)	130 years
To birth of Enosh (5:6)	105 "
To birth of Kenan (5:9)	90 "
To birth of Mahalalel (5:12)	70 "
To birth of Jared (5:15)	65 "
To birth of Enoch (5:18)	162 "
To birth of Methuselah (5:21)	65 "
To birth of Lamech (5:25)	187 "
To birth of Noah (5:28, 29)	182 "
To beginning of Flood (7:6)	600 "
Total	1,656 years

²⁷ Adding this figure 1,656 to 2,370 gives 4026 B.C.E., the Gregorian calendar year

24, 25. The Flood began in what calendar year, and how long was this before Abraham entered Canaan?
26, 27. (a) How long before the Flood was Adam created? In what year? (b) What indicates that Adam was created in the fall of the year?

in which Adam was created. Since man naturally began to count time with his own beginning, and since man's most ancient calendars started each year in the autumn, it is reasonable to assume that the first man Adam was created in the fall of the year.

²⁸ Thus, through a careful independent study by dedicated Bible scholars who have pursued the subject for a number of years, and who have not blindly followed some traditional chronological calculations of Christendom, we have arrived at a date for Adam's creation that is 22 years more distant in the past than Ussher's figure. This means time is running out two decades sooner than traditional chronology anticipates.

²⁹ After much of the mathematics and genealogies, really, of what benefit is this information to us today? Is it not all dead history, as uninteresting and profitless as walking through a cemetery copying old dates off tombstones? After all, why should we be any more interested in the date of Adam's creation than in the birth of King Tut? Well, for one thing, if 4,026 is added to 1,968 (allowing for the lack of a zero year between C.E. and B.C.E.) one gets a total of 5,993 years, come this autumn, since Adam's creation. That means, in the fall of the year 1975, a little over seven years from now (and not in 1997 as would be the case if Ussher's figures were correct), it will be 6,000 years since the creation of Adam, the father of all mankind!

ADAM CREATED AT CLOSE OF "SIXTH DAY"

³⁰ Are we to assume from this study that the battle of Armageddon will be all over by the autumn of 1975, and the long-looked-for thousand-year reign of Christ will begin by then? Possibly, but we wait to see how closely the seventh thousand-year period of man's existence coincides with the sabbathlike thousand-year reign of Christ. If these two periods run parallel with each other as to the calendar year, it will not be by mere chance or accident but will be according to Jehovah's loving and timely purposes. Our chronology, however, which is reasonably accurate (but admittedly not infallible), at the best only points to the autumn of 1975 as the end of 6,000 years of man's existence on earth. It does not necessarily mean that 1975 marks the end of the first 6,000 years of Jehovah's seventh creative "day." Why not? Because after his creation Adam lived some time during the "sixth day," which unknown amount of time would need to be subtracted from Adam's 930 years, to determine when the sixth seven-thousand-year period or "day" ended, and how long Adam lived into the "seventh day." And yet the end of that sixth creative "day" could end within the same Gregorian calendar year of Adam's creation. It may involve only a difference of weeks or months, not years.

³¹ In regard to Adam's creation it is good to read carefully what the Bible says. Moses in compiling the book of Genesis referred to written records or "histories" that predated the Flood. The first of these begins with Genesis 1:1 and ends at Genesis 2:4 with the words, "This is the history of the heavens and the earth . . . ." The second historical document begins with Genesis 2:5 and ends with verse two of chapter five. Hence we have two separate accounts of creation from slightly different points of view. In the second of these accounts, in Genesis 2:19, the original Hebrew verb translated "was forming" is in the progressive imperfect form. This does not mean that the animals and birds

28. How does this chronology differ from Ussher's in regard to Adam's creation?
29. Why be concerned with the date of Adam's creation?
30. What may occur before 1975, but what attitude should we take?
31. What do the first two chapters of Genesis disclose?

ing with the words of Jesus that "concerning that day and hour *nobody* knows, neither the angels of the heavens nor the Son, but only the Father." (Matt. 24:36) To the contrary, it is a time when one should be keenly aware that the end of this system of things is rapidly coming to its violent end. Make no mistake, it is sufficient that the Father himself *knows* both the "day and hour"!

¹⁶ Even if one cannot see beyond 1975, is this any reason to be less active? The apostles could not see even this far; they knew nothing about 1975. All they could see was a short time ahead in which to finish the work assigned to them. (1 Pet. 4:7) Hence, there was a ring of alarm and a cry of urgency in all their writings. (Acts 20:20; 2 Tim. 4:2) And rightly so. If they had delayed or dillydallied and had been complacent with the idea the end was some thousands of years off they would never have finished running the race set before them. No, they ran hard

and they ran fast, and they won! It was a life or death matter with them.—1 Cor. 9:24; 2 Tim. 4:7; Heb. 12:1.

³⁷ So too with Jehovah's faithful witnesses in this latter half of the twentieth century. They have the true Christian point of view. Their strenuous evangelistic activity is not something peculiar to this present decade. They have not dedicated their lives to serve Jehovah only until 1975. Christians have been running this way ever since Christ Jesus blazed the trail and commanded his disciples, "Follow me!" So keep this same mental attitude in you that was in Christ Jesus. Let nothing slow you down or cause you to tire and give out. Those who will flee Babylon the Great and this Satanic system of things are now running for their lives, headed for God's kingdom, and they will not stop at 1975. O no! They will keep on in this glorious way that leads to everlasting life, praising and serving Jehovah for ever and ever!

36. What helpful example did the apostles leave us in this regard?

37. So what will you be doing between now and 1975? And beyond that, what?

How 1st-CENTURY EVENTS ARE DATED in the 20th Century

IN THE previous two articles the truthfulness of the Bible's ancient history as far back as Adam's creation has been tested and proved. Any consideration of historical dates, however, would certainly be incomplete if it failed to locate Jesus' earthly ministry and that of his apostles on the stream of man's history, for, indeed, no one ever walked this earth who had a more profound effect on the lives and destinies of men and nations the world over.

² As already pointed out, neither our present Gregorian calendar, nor the Julian calendar, which it replaced less than 400 years ago, is in itself an adequate

1. Why is a further consideration of Bible dates important?

2. What is first necessary before first-century events can be dated?

A TIME TO

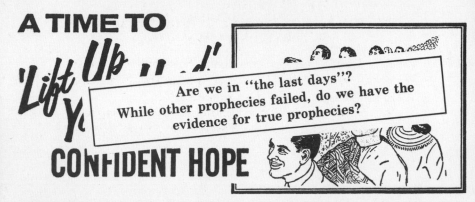

'Lift Up Your

CONFIDENT HOPE

Are we in "the last days"?
While other prophecies failed, do we have the evidence for true prophecies?

THE evidence that we are far along in the "last days" can be either good news or bad news to you, depending on the position you take. If you long to be free from a rule that has proved both unsatisfactory and unrighteous and that is torn more and more by discord and confusion; if you really love what is right and have a sincere desire to do the will of your Creator, then this evidence should make you rejoice. Why? Because, as Jesus Christ said: "As these things start to occur, raise yourselves erect and lift your heads up, because *your deliverance is getting near*."—Luke 21:28.

A perfect government, heaven-based and with heaven's blessing and heaven's power backing it up, will soon take complete control of this earth. In this way God will answer the prayer: "Let your kingdom come." What better news could there be?

Still some persons may say: "How can you be sure? Maybe it is later than many people think. But maybe it is not as late as some persons claim. People have been mistaken about these prophecies before."

The Difference

True, there have been those in times past who predicted an "end to the world,"

even announcing a specific date. Some have gathered groups of people with them and fled to the hills or withdrawn into their houses waiting for the end. Yet, nothing happened. The "end" did not come. They were guilty of false prophesying. Why? What was missing?

Missing was the full measure of evidence required in fulfillment of Bible prophecy. Missing from such people were God's truths and the evidence that he was guiding and using them.

But what about today? Today we have the evidence required, *all of it*. And it is overwhelming! All the many, many parts of the great sign of the "last days" are here, together with verifying Bible chronology.

Take a simple illustration: Suppose on a hot day at the beginning of summer, someone told you that winter was coming within a week because he had seen some trees without leaves. But those trees could have died from disease or age. So, by itself that would not be enough evidence that winter was approaching. Especially so when none of the other trees had shed their leaves, when the heat continued day after day, and when the calendar told you it was just the beginning of summer. You

4. THE WATCHTOWER, ITS PROPHECIES AND THE WORD OF GOD

Now that you have examined the prophecies of the Watchtower, you can apply the scriptural test to see if the Watchtower is a true or false prophet.

In order to summarize our findings, what was supposed to happen according to the Watchtower on the following dates?

> 1799
> 1874
> 1878
> 1914
> 1915
> 1918
> 1925
> 1929
> 1975

With Judgment Day honesty, we must ask ourselves, "Did any of the above prophecies fail to come about?" The only honest and faithful answer is, "All of them failed to be fulfilled. They were all *false* prophecies."

What verdict did Moses and Jesus tell us to pass on the Watchtower?

Answer: The Watchtower is a false prophet (Deut. 18:22). It is not God's organization and it does not speak in YHWH's name (Deut. 18:20). We should not be afraid of it or even respect it (Deut. 18:22). We must quickly take our stand with Moses and Jesus in rejecting the Watchtower as a false prophet (Matt. 7:15).

BUT?

If the Watchtower is a false prophet and cannot be

trusted but must be rejected, to where shall we turn?

  Answer: Not to any human organization or society but to the eternal Word of God, the Holy Scriptures. The Bible is to be the only ultimate religious authority. It can be trusted, for it is the Word of God.

WHAT THEN?

You must reexamine everything the Watchtower has taught you. You must not be afraid of the Watchtower but study the Bible without their books and magazines. Don't let a false prophet tell you what the Bible says. You must learn to interpret the Bible for yourself.

Are you willing to trust God and His Word? Are you going to obey Moses and Jesus Christ to beware of the false prophet called the Watchtower? What are you going to do?

Part 3

IS JESUS CHRIST YHWH?

PREFACE

The importance of this subject warrants the utmost care in selecting a correct translation of the Bible. The following translations are recommended as being generally faithful to the Hebrew and Greek:

King James Version
American Standard, 1901 (Watchtower Edition)
New American Standard Bible (Creation House)
The Bible in Living English (Watchtower Edition)
New International Version (Zondervan Bible
    Publishers)

INTRODUCTION

The following workbook is designed to enable any serious student of the Bible to investigate in great detail what the Bible teaches on the subject of the deity or godhood of Jesus Christ. It is expected that the reader will be faithful in looking up all the scripture passages, in examining the context of each passage and in having a willing and open mind to accept whatever the Bible teaches even if it contradicts his previous religious convictions. In John 7:17, Jesus reminds us that religious truth can be obtained only by those who approach the subject with a willing attitude. Jesus said:

If any man is willing to do his will, he shall know of the teaching, whether it is of God or whether I speak from myself.

PRELIMINARY QUESTIONS

1. Is it scripturally possible for God to take upon himself *human* nature and to become a man in every sense of the word? (Mark 10:27; Ps. 135:6; Job 42:2; Dan. 4:34-35).

The reader must acknowledge that "all things are possible with God" (Mark 10:27). Thus, we must admit at the very outset of our study that *it is possible for God to be incarnate in human form*. To approach the deity of Christ with the assumption or presupposition that it is *not* possible for Christ to be deity is to reveal a lack of openness to the Scriptures and a rationalistic attitude which says, "Don't confuse me with the facts. My mind is already made up." We should not limit what God can or cannot do simply on the basis of what *we* think He can or cannot do. Any theology which tells God that He cannot do a certain thing is not only poor theology, but it also borders on being blasphemy.

2. Literally speaking, is there only *one* God or are there *many* gods? Does the Bible teach monotheism or polytheism? (Isa. 43:10, 11; 44:6, 7; 45:5, 6, 21-23; 46:9; Acts 19:26; Gal. 4:8). _____

3. Even though literally speaking there is only one true God and the "gods" of the heathen are nothing but man-made idols (Ps. 115:1-8), the word "god" was at times used in a figurative manner or sense to describe someone or something which had a godlike function. Thus, Moses

was to function as a godlike judge over Pharaoh (Ex. 4:16). Satan is figuratively called "the god of this age" (2 Cor. 4:4). The judges over Israel were called *Elohim*, that is, "gods" in Ex. 21:6; 22:8, 9, etc., because like God, they held the power of life and death over men. While Moses, the judges, angels and even Satan himself are, at times, called "god" in a figurative sense, are they ever said to be God by nature? _____

_____

Are we ever told to bow before them and give them divine worship? _____

Are we told to pray to them? _____

Are we ever told to place our ultimate faith, hope, trust, and love in them? _____

Are the divine characteristics such as eternity or omnipresence ever attributed to them? _____

While they may have been called *Elohim* (God), were they ever called *YHWH* (Jehovah)? _____

4. Since there is only one true God, will this God share His glory with anyone else? (Isa. 42:8) _____

5. Can we worship any created being or thing? or does the Bible teach that we are to worship God alone? (Deut. 6:13) _____

OLD TESTAMENT SURVEY

1. Did YHWH ever come down to earth and manifest himself to people in the form of a man? (Gen. 18:1-5, 13, 17, 22; 32:24-30; cf. 35:1-3, 9-13; Ex. 24:9-11; Isa. 6:1-9) _____

2. When YHWH was in His human form, did men actually see and touch Him? (Gen. 16:13; 18:1-5; 32:24-30; Ex. 24:9-11; Isa. 6:1-9) _____

3. While Ex. 34:20 states that to see God in His absolute glory would mean instant death, evidently men could see YHWH in His human form. Thus, Moses could see

YHWH's back without dying (Ex. 33:18-23). Abraham could wash YHWH's feet (Gen. 18:1-4), and Jacob could wrestle with YHWH's body (Gen. 32:30; 35:1-15; Ex. 3:6). And Isaiah escaped death even though he saw YHWH with his own eyes (Isa. 6:5).

4. The key to unlock these mysterious appearances of YHWH in human form is found in John 12:37-43. In this passage the Apostle John clearly points out that the YHWH who appeared to Isaiah as "Jehovah of Armies" (Isa. 6:1-5) was _____ in His preincarnate glory. Thus whenever YHWH appeared in His human form, it was probably _____ that men saw and touched.

5. In this light, who was probably YHWH/man who visited Abraham in Gen. 18? (John 8:56-59) _____

6. How many Jehovah's are mentioned in Gen. 19:24?___ Who was probably the YHWH/man on earth who rained fire upon Sodom from the YHWH who was in heaven? (Gen. 18:33; cf. 19:24) _____

7. Who was the YHWH/man who wrestled with Jacob? (Gen. 32:30; cf. Ex. 3:6) _____

8. Since the "God of Jacob" is the One with whom Jacob wrestled, and is later identified in Ex. 3:6 as YHWH, who could this God/Man be? (Ex. 3:6; cf. Gen. 35:2-13) _____ The most logical identification of YHWH/man of the Old Testament is _____ in His preincarnate glory.

9. God called himself in Ex. 3:13, 14, by the name of _____. In the New Testament, who also claimed this divine name? (John 8:58, 59) _____

10. Now if Christ was only called *Elohim* (god) in a figurative sense like Moses or Satan, it would not be necessary to believe that He is God in His nature. But Jesus is called *YHWH* and is different in every way from the figurative "gods."
Are we told to worship Jesus? (Ps. 2:12) _____

Did the Old Testament saints worship Jesus? (Gen. 32:30; cf. 35:1-15; Isa. 6:1-5; Ex. 24:1, 9-11) _____

Are we told to put our trust, faith, and love in Jesus? (Ps. 2:12) _____

Are divine attributes given to Him? (Micah 5:2; Isa. 9:6) _____

Is He called YHWH? (Isa. 6:5; cf. John 12:41) _____

11. In the following Old Testament passages, we find that YHWH is spoken of in either direct or indirect language. These passages are either quoted or alluded to in the New Testament. Check and see if the New Testament writers applied the YHWH Old Testament passages directly to Jesus. If they did this, it is obvious that they felt that the YHWH of the Old Testament is the Jesus of the New Testament. After each series of scriptures, write out the particular YHWH name, title or function that is attributed to Jesus Christ.

   a. Ps. 23:1; Isa. 40:1-11; cf. John 10:1-14; Heb. 13:20, 1 Pet. 2:25; 5:4. _____

   b. Ps. 50:1-6; cf. 2 Thess. 1:7-10. _____

   c. Ps. 68:15-18; cf. Eph. 4:8. _____

   d. Ps. 102:1, 12, 25-27; cf. Heb. 1:10-12. _____

   e. Isa. 8:12-15; cf. 1 Pet. 2:8. _____

   f. Isa. 40:3, 9, 10, 11; cf. John 1:23; Rev. 22:12. _____

   g. Isa. 43:3; cf. Acts 3:14. _____

   h. Isa. 44:6; cf. Rev. 1:7, 8, 17, 18; 2:8; 22:13. _____

   i. Isa. 45:22, 23; cf. Rom. 14:9-12; cf. 2 Cor. 5:10; Phil. 2:10. _____

   j. Isa. 62:11, 12; cf. Rev. 22:12. _____

   k. Jer. 11:20; 17:10; 20:12; cf. Rev. 2:23. _____

   l. Jer. 23:6; Zech. 3:8; 6:12; Mal. 3:1, 2; cf. Matt. 11:10. _____

   m. Joel 2:32; cf. Rom. 10:9-15. _____

   n. Zech. 12:10; cf. John 19:37. _____

12. Not only is Jesus identified as the YHWH of the Old

Testament, but He is also given other names of God. After each passage, write out the names or titles given to Christ.

a. Gen. 18:3; cf. Acts 10:36. _____
b. Gen. 18:25; cf. 2 Tim. 4:1, 8. _____
c. Gen. 32:30; cf. John 1:1. _____
d. Gen. 35:11; cf. Gen. 35:1. _____
e. Ex. 3:14; cf. John 8:58. _____
f. Ps. 23:1; cf. John 10:14. _____
g. Ps. 45:6; cf. Heb. 1:8. _____
h. Isa. 7:14; cf. Matt. 1:23. _____
i. Isa. 9:6; cf. Luke 1:31-33. _____

Note: In the Hebrew of Isa. 9:6, "Mighty God" appears without the definite article. But this is also true in such places as Isa. 10:21; 49:26. Since YHWH is called "Mighty God" without the definite article in Isa. 10:20-21, the absence of the article cannot be interpreted to show that YHWH is just "a god" in a figurative sense. In the same way, neither can the absence of the article in Isa. 9:6 reduce Jesus to "a god." But the comparison between Isa. 9:6 and Isa. 10:20-21 demonstrates that Jesus is the YHWH who is the "Mighty God." After all, there cannot be two "Mighty Gods," for there is only one God (Isa. 43:10).

There is also an irrefutable scriptural logic behind the proposition that Jesus is YHWH. In logic, the following syllogism is *always valid*:

$$A > B \qquad a = b$$
$$\underline{B > C \text{ or } b = c}$$
$$A > C \qquad a = c$$

In the same way, the teaching of Scripture can be arranged in conformity to the above syllogism.

>Jesus is "Mighty God" (Isa. 9:6)
>"Mighty God" is YHWH (Isa. 10:20-21)
>Jesus is YHWH

The logical sequence cannot be shown to be invalid. The conclusion is automatic and irrefutable.

    j. Isa. 10:20; cf. Acts 3:14. _____

    k. Isa. 44:6; cf. Rev. 22:12-16 (v. 13). _____

13. The Old Testament prophesied that while Christ was to be born in Bethlehem, His origin should be traced back to eternity itself. How does Micah 5:2 describe this origin of Christ? _____

_____

Note: The words "from everlasting" are also used to describe the origin of YHWH in Ps. 90:1, 2.
Did YHWH have a beginning? _____
How does Ps. 90:2 express the eternity of YHWH? _____

Since the same Hebrew word is used in Micah 5:2 as found in Ps. 90:2, what does this tell us about Christ? _____

_____

CONCLUSION

In the Old Testament the Messiah is clearly prophesied as the coming of YHWH in human form to redeem a lost and sinful humanity (Isa. 40:1, 9-11). To prepare the way for the incarnation of YHWH, He appeared in human form on many occasions so that the people of God would be prepared to see and touch the living God when He came to die on the cross (Zech. 12:10). The Messiah is none other than YHWH incarnate as a human being.

NEW TESTAMENT SURVEY

1. At the very outset of the New Testament, John the Baptist is sent to prepare the way for the coming of _____; (Isa. 40:3, 10; cf. Matt. 3:1-3; Luke 1:76). Granted that John the Baptist clearly came to prepare the way for the coming of YHWH, did he ever identify Jesus as the One of whom he spoke? (John 1:23, 30)

_____

2. The angel who announced the incarnation to Mary instructed her that her child would be "Immanuel" (Matt. 1:23). What does this name mean?

_____

3. When the beginning began, was the Word (Christ) already existing in eternity itself? (John 1:1) _____

4. John identifies this eternal Word as _____ in John 1:1.

   Note: It is grammatically impossible to translate John 1:1 as "the Word was a god." The absence of the definite article in John 1:1 does not mean "a god" should be translated in such places. John calls Christ "God" to identify the divine nature of the Word.

5. Who is the Creator of the universe? (John 1:3; Col. 1:16, 17; Heb. 1:10-12, 2:10) _____

6. John 1:18 primarily concerns two persons. Who are they? _____

7. We are told in John 1:18 that no one has ever seen the *Father* in His own absolute and essential glory. Yet, at the same time, we are told that Christ, here called "the unique God," has fully revealed the Father. Thus, John 1:18 says that no one ever saw God the Father but they have seen God the Son.

   Note: The KJV's "only begotten Son" comes from an error in the received text. The proper Greek text reads "only God" and is being rendered so in most modern versions. That the Greek word *monogenes* means "unique" or "only" and not "created" can be established by any Greek lexicon or by an examination of Heb. 11:17 where Isaac is called Abraham's *monogenes* son. Since Abraham had many sons he had begotten (Gen. 16:15; 25:6), Isaac was not the only "created" son. But Isaac was the "unique" son, being the heir of all things (Gen. 25:5). Thus *monogenes* means "unique" or "only one of its kind."

8. John 1:18 gives us the key to understand the appearances of YHWH in human form in the Old Testament. The *Jehovah God* who appeared to Abraham, Jacob, Moses, Isaiah, etc., was none other than Jesus Christ in His pre-incarnate state. The YHWH of the Old Testament is the same person whom the New Testament calls *Jesus Christ.*

9. When the Jews sought to kill Jesus, the Apostle John tells us that their primary reason was that Jesus claimed that God was His Father in a unique sense not shared with any other being. Then John adds his own understanding of what Jesus meant when he said that God was His own Father. What did John say? (John 5:18). _____

   _____

10. Having stated that Jesus was "equal with God" the Father in John 5:18, this equality is further expanded in John 5:23. We are to give equal _____ to the Father and to the Son. The words "even as" reveal that all worship and _____ we show to the Father must also equally be given to Jesus Christ. If someone does not give Christ equal honor with the Father, what does John give as the consequences in the second half of verse 23? _____

   _____

11. In John 10:31. the Jews attempted to stone Jesus. Why did they do this? (v. 30) _____

_____

12. Since the Jews would not have been upset if Jesus simply meant "I and my Father are one in purpose and in work," what was their understanding of Jesus' words "I and My Father are One"? (v. 33) _____

_____

Thus, the Jews clearly saw that Christ was claiming to be YHWH. Just as they tried to stone Him for what they felt was blasphemy in John 10:31, what did they do when Jesus called himself YHWH's name "I AM" in John 8:58, 59? _____

_____

13. If you do not believe that Jesus is "I AM," what will happen to you? (John 8:24) _____

14. After Christ was raised from the dead, He proved His bodily resurrection to doubting Thomas by letting him see and handle the wounds on His body which He received on the cross (John 20:27). Thomas was convinced of Christ's bodily resurrection and, also, he spoke to Jesus directly calling Him various names. The words "unto him" in verse 28 reveal that Thomas was not simply making an exclamation into the air but what he said must be applied "unto him," that is, Christ Jesus himself. What did Thomas call Christ? (v. 28) _____

15. Did Jesus rebuke Thomas for taking God's name in vain or attributing to Him that which belongs only to God the Father? (v. 29) _____
Jesus approved of Thomas' words because He is Thomas' Lord and God.

16. In the New Testament, did angels allow themselves to be worshipped by men? (Rev. 22:8, 9; cf. Col. 2:18).

_____

17. Did the Father ever say to angels "you are my Son"?

(Heb. 1:5) _____

18. Whom do the angels worship? (Heb. 1:6) _____

19. When Jesus appeared to Isaiah as YHWH in human form, what were the seraphim doing? (Isa. 6:1-5)

_____

20. Is it therefore possible for Christ to be only an angel?

_____

21. Should men be worshipped? (Acts 14:11-18) _____

22. Whom did the disciples and the apostles worship? (Matt. 2:2, 11; 8:2; 9:18; 14:33; 28:9, 17; Luke 24:52; John 9:38; 1 Cor. 1:2) _____

_____

23. In Acts 20:28, whose blood purchased the church?

_____

24. According to Rom. 9:5, who is "over all" and "God blessed forever"? _____

25. Who is the "Rock" of Israel? (Deut. 32:1-4) _____
What did the people of Israel do to the Rock YHWH? (Deut. 32:15-18) _____

26. According to 1 Cor. 10:1-4, who was the Rock of Israel (YHWH) referred to in the Old Testament? _____

27. In whom does "the fulness of deity dwell in bodily form"? (Col. 2:9) _____

28. In Titus 2:13, who is called "our great God and Saviour"? _____

29. Who is called the same thing in 2 Pet. 1:1? _____

30. Who is the true God and eternal life in 1 John 5:20?

_____

31. Did the Father share His glory with the Son? (John 17:5) _____
Would the Father share His glory with a created being? (Isa. 42:8) _____
What conclusion does this naturally lead to? _____

_____

32. In Col. 1:16, we are told that Christ created all _____. All _____ were created _____ Him

and _____ Him. (v. 16) We are also told in verse 17 that Jesus Christ existed _____ all _____ came into being. He is the Sovereign Sustainer of the universe because He "holds together" or "upholds" all _____ (v. 16).

33. Since the Bible states quite clearly that Christ created *all things* and sustains *all things*, it is obvious that He himself cannot be a _____, that is, a created being. Colossians 1 shows us that Christ is the Creator and not a creature. He is the Sustainer and not a dependent being.

  Note: The New World Translation has "all *other* things" instead of "all things." The Greek does not have the word "other" in the text. The verse simply says that Christ created "all things."

34. The book of Hebrews demonstrates the superiority of Christ in His person and in His work over that of the Old Testament economy. The key word in the book of Hebrews is "_____" (1:4; 7:19, 22; 8:6; 9:23; 12:24). This word points out the qualitative superiority of Christ's nature. He is, by nature, in terms of His being better than anyone and anything else in the universe.

  a. Heb. 1:1-3 shows us that Christ's revelation of the Father is "better" than the Old Testament revelation given by the _____.

  b. Heb. 1:4 states that Christ is "better" (superior in His being) to the _____. The reasons why Christ cannot be viewed as an angel are as follows:
    1. He inherited a better _____ (v. 4).
    2. The Father never at any time ever said to any angel _____ _____ (v. 5).
    3. Instead of the angels viewing Christ as an equal or just an angel like them, the Father command-

ed that the angels should _____ Christ to show that Jesus is superior to them (v. 6).

4. The Father calls the angels _____ and His ministers _____ (v. 7).

5. In contrast to what He calls the angels, the Father calls Christ _____ when He said, "Thy throne, O _____, is forever and ever" in verse 8.

   Note: Some have tried to translate the Greek as "your throne is God." But this does not follow the actual wording of the verse in the Greek text, and the picture of the Father being sat upon as someone's chair does not fit the context of the chapter. Also, it would imply that the Son is "better" than the Father, for it is only obvious that the person who sits on a chair is superior to that chair. The whole point of the passage is to show that the Son is "better," that is, superior to the angels. He is superior because He is God. The Father can call Christ "God" in Heb. 1:8 just as the Son calls the Father "God" in John 5:18.

6. After the Father calls Christ _____ in verse 8, He calls Him _____ in verse 10. Both verses are quotations from the Old Testament. The word "Lord" in verse 10 comes from Psalm 102. The exact name of God that is used in Psalm 102 is _____ (Ps. 102:1, 2, 25-27). Thus the Father not only calls Christ "God" but also _____. The YHWH of Psalm 102 is the _____ of Heb. 1:8-12.

7. According to Ps. 102:25-27, who created the world? _____
   To what natural and logical conclusion do the above answers lead you? _____

8. According to Ps. 102:26 and Heb. 1:11, 12, all created things are temporary and not eternal. Everything will perish. But in contrast to the temporary character of created reality, YHWH remains the same (Ps. 102:26, 27). In the Old Testament YHWH declared in Mal. 3:6, "I, YHWH, do not _____." These classic Old Testament YHWH passages are applied without hesitation to Jesus Christ. Christ is "the _____ yesterday, today, and _____" (Heb. 13:8). The Father points this out in Heb. 1:11, 12. He said that created things will "_____" (v. 12). The context will allow only the one interpretation that Christ is superior to the angels because He is the eternal YHWH who created all things. While all created things decay and ultimately come to an end, Christ remains ever the same.

9. The last argument of the author of Hebrews to prove that Christ is superior to the angels is found in 1:13, 14. Did the Father ever at any time ask an angel to sit at His right hand? _____ To sit at the Father's right hand is to share in the Father's glory and dominion. Did the Father ever say to any angel, "Sit at my right hand" while *I* will serve *you* by "making your enemies your footstool"? _____ While the Son sits enthroned next to the Father, with the Father himself bringing honor and glory to the Son by subduing His enemies, the angels are but "ministering _____," sent forth to minister to " _____ ."

CONCLUSION

Jesus Christ is both God and Man. He is YHWH incarnate as a human being. The New Testament writers without hesitation took the classic YHWH Old Testament passages and applied them directly to Christ. Jesus is given divine titles and worshipped as deity by angels and by men. It is impossible to escape the deity of Christ and do justice to the New Testament Scriptures.

WHO IS GOD?

God Is a Spirit

ST. JOHN . 4 23, 24
ACTS 7.48, 49
ACTS 17 24-28
PSA. 139:11, 12
I KINGS 8 27
JER. 23 21-27

There Is But One God

DEUT. 6:4-9
MARK 12:28-34
MAL. 2 10
ISA. 44:6-8
ISA. 45:2-6, 23
ISA. 46:8, 9
I COR. 8.4-6
EPH. 4:5, 6
I TIM. 2:5
JAMES 2:19
REV. 4:2, 3
MAL. 1:6

[Central circular diagram with radiating sections pointing to center "ONE GOD"]

Sections (clockwise from top):

GOD THE CREATOR
GEN. . . 1:1
GEN. . . 2:7
JOB . . . 93:4
PSA. . . 33:6
PSA. .104:30
ISA. . 90:28
ISA. 44:24
ISA 45:11-18
MAL. 2:10
ONE CREATOR

GOD THE REDEEMER AND SAVIOUR
PSA. 78:34,35
ISA. . 47:4
ISA. . 48:6
ISA. . 43:3,11
ISA. 49:21
PSA. 49:20
LUKE 1:46-47
ONE SAVIOUR

GOD THE SHEPHERD
PSA. . 23
ISA. 40:10,11
PSA. 100
ONE SHEPHERD

GOD THE KING
PSA. . 47
PSA. . 95:3
PSA. 93:10-15
ISA. 44:6
JER. 10:10
ZACH.14:9
ONE KING

GOD THE I AM AND I AM HE
EXOD. 3:13,14
"I AM HE"
ISA. 43:10,11,25
ONE I AM
ONE I AM HE

GOD FIRST AND LAST
ISA. . 41:4
ISA. 43:10,11
ISA. . 44:6,8
ONE FIRST AND LAST

GOD THE ROCK
DEUT. 32:4
2 SAM. 22:32
PSA. . 18:2
PSA. . 78:35
PSA. 89:26
PSA. 92:10,11
ISA.
ONE ROCK

GOD IS COMING
ZACH.14:45
ITHESS.4:13-18
REV. 19:11,16
PSA. 50:1-6
ONE IS COMING

JESUS THE CREATOR
JOHN. 1:10
I COR. 8:6
EPH. 3:9
COL. 1:12-17
HEB. 1:8-12
REV. 4:8-11
REV. 10:6
REV. 14:6,7
REV. 21:5-7
REV. 22:3
REV. 7:17
ONE CREATOR

JESUS REDEEMER AND SAVIOUR
JOHN 4:42
ACTS 13:23
ACTS 5:31
GAL. 3:13
LUKE 2:11
JOHN. 3:16,17
ACTS 4:10-12
PHIL. 3:20
I TIM. 1:1
I TIM. 4:10
TITU. 1:3
TITU. 2:10,13
I PET. 1:18,19
JUDE 25
ONE SAVIOUR

JESUS THE SHEPHERD
JOHN 10:11-14
I PET 2:20,25
HEB. 13:20
2 PET. 5:4
ONE SHEPHERD

JESUS THE KING
MATT. 2:1-6
LUKE 19:32-38
LUKE 23:3
JOHN. 18:37
JOHN. 19:21
JOHN. 6:13-14
REV. 15:1
REV. 19:11-16
ONE KING

JESUS THE I AM AND I AM HE
JOHN 18:5-8
REV. 1:17-8
JOHN 8:24-28
ONE I AM HE
ONE I AM

JESUS FIRST AND LAST
REV. 1:17
REV. 22:13
ONE FIRST AND LAST

JESUS THE ROCK
MATT. 16:17-19
ISA. 28:16
ACTS 4:11-12
I COR. 10: 4
NUM. 20:1-11
EPH. 2:20,22
I PET. 2:6-8
ONE ROCK

JESUS IS COMING
I THESS. 3:11-13
MATT. 25:31,46
TITUS 2:11-13
ONE IS COMING

ONE GOD

Jesus Is God

ISA. 7:14
ISA. 9 6
MAL. 2:10
GEN. 1 1
ZACH. 14 9
ISA. 43 10
EXOD. 3 13-15

He Is Man

MATT. 1:23
I TIM. 3 16
II COR. 5 19
JOHN 12 44, 45
JOHN 14 6-10
JOHN 10:30-33
JOHN 8 21, 24-28
JOHN 8 56-58
JOHN 1 10

-94-

This chart is available from Help Jesus, Box 2212, Station R, Kelowna, B.C., Canada.

SOURCE MATERIAL USED IN THIS BOOK

Part 2, pp. 31-34, *The Watchtower*, March 15, 1972, pp. 186-190.

pp. 35-38, *The Watchtower*, April 1, 1972, pp. 197-200.

p. 39, *Riches*, The Watchtower Bible and Tract Society, Brooklyn, N.Y., 1936.

pp. 41-42, *Zion's Watchtower*, Pittsburgh, Pa., Jan. 1886, Vol. VII, No. 5, p. 817.

pp. 43-44, *The Time Is at Hand*, Watchtower Bible and Tract Society, Allegheny, Pa., 1897, pp. 620, 621.

pp. 45-46, *Zion's Watchtower*, Jan. 15, 1892, pp. 21-23.

pp. 47-48, *The Day of Vengeance*, Watchtower Bible and Tract Society, Allegheny, Pa., 1897, pp. 620-621.

pp. 49-50, *The New Creation*, Watchtower Bible and Tract Society, Brooklyn, N.Y., 1904, pp. 578-579.

pp. 51-52, *The Time Is at Hand*, Watchtower Bible and Tract Society, Brooklyn, N.Y., 1912, pp. 76-78.

p. 53, *The Watchtower*, Sept. 1, 1914, pp. 261-263.

p. 54-55, *New York Times*, N.Y., Monday, Oct. 5, 1914, p. 8.

pp. 56-57, *The Watchtower*, April 1, 1915, pp. 101-102.

p. 58, *The Watchtower*, Sept. 1, 1916, pp. 265-266.

pp. 59-60, *The Finished Mystery*, Watchtower Bible and Tract Society, Brooklyn, N.Y., 1917, pp. 484-485.

pp. 61-63, *Millions Now Living Will Never Die*, Watchtower Bible and Tract Society, Brooklyn, N.Y., 1920, pp. 88-91.

p. 64, *The Watchtower*, Sept. 1, 1922.

p. 65, *The Watchtower*, May 2, p. 100.

p. 66, *The Watchtower*, Jan. 1, 1925, Vol. XLVI, No. 1, p. 3.

pp. 67-74, *Creation*, Watchtower Bible and Tract Society, Brooklyn, N.Y., 1927, pp. 289, 294-295, 298-299, 306-309.

pp. 75-76, *Prophecy*, Watchtower Bible and Tract Society, Brooklyn, N.Y., 1929, pp. 64-65.

pp. 77-78, *Salvation*, Watchtower Bible and Tract Society, Brooklyn, N.Y., 1929, pp. 311-312.

pp. 79-80, *Vindication*, Watchtower Bible and Tract Society, Brooklyn, N.Y., 1931, pp. 338-339.

pp. 81-82, *Life Everlasting—In Freedom of the Sons of God*, Watchtower Bible and Tract Society, Brooklyn, N.Y., 1966, pp. 29-30.

p. 83, *Kingdom Ministry*, May, 1974, p. 3.

pp. 84-87, *The Watchtower*, August 15, 1968, pp. 494, 498-499, 501.

p. 88, *Awake*, Oct. 8, 1968, p. 23.